POPULAR EDUCATION;

OR,

THE NORMAL SCHOOL MANUAL:

CONTAINING

PRACTICAL SUGGESTIONS FOR DAILY AND SUNDAY SCHOOL TEACHERS.

IN A SERIES OF LETTERS.

BY

HENRY DUNN,

SECRETARY TO THE BRITISH AND FOREIGN SCHOOL SOCIETY.

LONDON:
PUBLISHED BY THE SUNDAY SCHOOL UNION,
NO. 60, PATERNOSTER ROW.

1837.

London : J. Rider, Printer, 14, Bartholomew Close.

CONTENTS.

LETTER I.

OBJECT OF THE BOOK. — A Manual wanted. — Prevailing Defect in Works on Education. — Principles rather than Methods to be studied. — German and American Writers. — Schools oo frequently the last Hope of the Unfortunate. — Sunday Schools. — Missionaries. — Henry Meyer. — Wordsworth.

LETTER II.

PLEASANTNESS OF TEACHING. — Sir Walter Scott. — Force and Influence. — Mr. Abbott. — Benevolence. — Dr. Dwight. — Faith in Early Instruction. — Didaktik. — Competent Information. — Dr. Reid. — Eminent Sunday School Teachers. — Fellenberg. — Fenelon.

LETTER III.

GOVERNMENT. — Dr. Johnson. — Arbitrary Character of School Government. — Locke. — Lord Mansfield. — Dr. Bryce. — Good Order. — Inflexible Determination. — Spirit of the

CONTENTS.

Saviour. — Hooker. — Tones of the Voice. — Moral Suasion. — Claims of Authority. — The Custom-house Officer. — Moral Influence of the absent Teacher. — Habitual Ascendancy. — Ministers of the Gospel. — Practical Remarks. — Public Opinion. — Strict Impartiality. — Respect for Youthful Feelings. — Power of Rebuke. — The Tones of Friendship. — Judicious Praise. — The Two Commanders. — Captain Basil Hall. — Leaders and Demagogues. — Uniformity. — Salzmann. — Joseph Lancaster. — Co-operation of Parents. — New Scholars. — Cobbett. — Education of the Ox. — Confirmed Depravity. — Order in Sunday Schools. — Peculiar Difficulties.

LETTER IV.

THE MONITORIAL SYSTEM. — Father Girard. — Professor Pillans. — Mr. Wood. — Dr. Johnson. — Superiority over Adults as subordinate Instructors. — Moral Advantages. — Automaton Schoolmasters. — German Prejudices. — Characteristics of good Monitors. — Selection and Training. — Delegation of Authority. — Mr. Crossley. — Unfaithfulness. — Noise.

LETTER V.

DIDAKTIK. — Definitions. — Analogy between Teaching and Medicine. — Dr. Thomas Brown. — The young Lazzaroni. — *The Alphabet.* — Wood, Pillans, and Jacotot. — *Spelling.* — Woodbridge, Parkhurst, and Thayer. — Plan at the Borough Road School. — *Reading.* — Nature. — Unmeaning Combinations. — Conversational Tones and Emphases. — Rapidity and Loudness. — Quantity. — *Interrogation.* — Miss Hamilton. — Visible Illustrations. — Specimens. —

Indians at Philadelphia. — Evidence of Testimony. — Mr. Hume. — Latin and Greek roots. — *Incidental Teaching.* — Cramming. — Professor Pillans. — Beattie. — The Borough Road School. — *Writing.* — Hints on Classification and other matters. — *Arithmetic.* — Sensible Objects. — Abstractions. — Reasons and Explanations. — Colburn's Lecture. — The Decimal Ratio. — Old Fuller's Precept. — Correctness and Dispatch. — Rapid Questioning. — Weariness. — *Grammar.* — William Cobbett. — Rules and Definitions. — Missionaries and Barbarians. — Modes of Teaching. — *Geography.* — Beginning at Home. — Maps. — Woodbridge's Lecture. — Other branches. — Sale of Water. — Linear Drawing. — Composition. — Mental Habits. — Importance of Accuracy. — Memory. — Attention. — The South-American Indian. — Association. — Dr. Abercrombie. — Reason. — Enlarged Course of Instruction. — The Penobscot Indians. — Favourite Studies. — New and Improved Methods. — Pestalozzi. — Fellenberg. — Jacotot. — The Indolent. — The Precocious. — Experience at Hofwyl. — Dr. Spurzheim. — Intellectual Hot-houses. — Zerah Colburn. — The Christian Observer. — Evelyn's Child. — Sunday Schools.

LETTER VI.

REWARDS ANL PUNISHMENTS. — Fellenberg. — Dr. Bryce. — Emulation. — Professor Stuart. — Advantages of Competition. — The selfish. — The vain. — The self-complacent. — Pleasant Memorials. — Mr. Hall's Lectures. — Retrospective Associations. — Salzmann's Art of Mis-education. — Little Charlotte. — The Duke of Marlborough and Prince Eugene. — Beccaria. — Corporal Punishments. — Fellenberg, Pillans, and Wood. — General Observations. — Denzel's Seven Suggestions.

LETTER VII.

MORAL AND RELIGIOUS INFLUENCE. — Coleridge. — Idle Fears. — Exclusive Views. — Human Nature. — Moral Education. — Affection. — The Bible. — Fellenberg. — Illustrations from Nature. — Elementary Truths. — The Being of God. — Cause and Effect. — Immortality of the Soul. — Gallaudet. — Future Retribution. — Conscience. — Opportunities. — Doctrines. — Theological Prating. — Habits. — Cleanliness. — Pleasant Associations. — The Country Schoolmaster. — Self-denial. — Intemperance. — Economy. — Savings Banks. — Gentleness. — Regard for Life. — Captain Back. — Stories. — Humanity to Brutes. — Playmates. — Fagging. — Benevolence. — Active Effort. — Respect for Women. — The Beautiful. — Pedestrian Excursions. — Natural Scenery. — Sir James Mackintosh. — Vocal Music. — Luther. — Continental Peasantry. — Traveller in Switzerland. — Truth. — Lord Bacon. — Lying. — Association. — Incidental Opportunities. — The Teacher a Judge. — Monitorial Schools. — Mimicry of Providence. — Opposing Influences. — Parents. — Association of Teachers. — Interesting Facts. — Flattery of Visitors. — Devotional Exercises. — Private Prayer. — The great Encouragement.

LETTER VIII.

MORAL AND INTELLECTUAL HABITS OF A TEACHER. — Mothers and Schoolmasters. — Self-control. — Debt. — Personal Neatness. — Tobacco and Snuff. — Mental Habits. — Intercourse with a Committee. — Private Studies. — Elements. — The Virginian Philanthropists. — Principles. — Professor Jardine. — Art of Teaching. — Essential Qualifications.

CONTENTS. vii

— The External World. — Mental Philosophy. — Dugald Stewart. — Books on Education. — Clearness and Precision. — Attention. — Imagination. — Immoral Writings. — Study. — Normal School of Pyritz. — Young People. — Salzmann. — Health and Cheerfulness. — Evening Teaching. — Abbott. — Plan. — Private Devotion. — Coleridge.

LETTER IX.

DUTIES OF A COMMITTEE. — The School Room. — Materials for Teaching. — The Teacher. — Early Attendance. — Good Order. — Adherence to a System. — Children. — Sunday Schools and Examinations. — Sympathy. — Discouragements. — Multiplicity of Objects. — Moral Responsibility for others. — Daily Irritations. — Station in Society. — Pecuniary Difficulties. — Finances. — Reports. — Collection of Subscriptions. — Results. — Enemies and Friends. — Interest in Elder Children. — Meetings of Old Scholars. — Gratifying Facts. — General Result.

POPULAR EDUCATION;

OR,

PRACTICAL HINTS ON TEACHING.

LETTER I.   TO A FRIEND.

OBJECT OF THE WORK.

1. VARIOUS motives, my dear friend, have influenced me in determining, without further delay, to attempt the preparation of a small volume for the use of teachers. It is just seven years to day* since I entered upon my present engagements, and became *exclusively* devoted to the furtherance of popular education in connexion with the British and Foreign School Society. Can I commemorate the completion of this period better, or express my gratitude to the Author of all good for the mercies of seven happy years more suitably, than by endeavouring to gather up, for the benefit of others, the fruit which, in that time, one would suppose,

* Jan. 1, 1836, the date of the first letter.

experience must have dropped into the lap even of the most unobservant? I know not why I should be ashamed to confess, that the idea of possessing such a memorial of our pleasant intercourse, has not been without its weight, in adjusting the balance of conflicting views and feelings, with regard to the *immediate* fulfilment of the task I have undertaken.

2. That a manual of this description is wanted, I have long been convinced. Gathered, as elementary teachers generally are, from the humbler walks of society; previously engaged, for the most part, in occupations allowing but little time for self improvement; without books, and unable to purchase them; it is not to be expected that they should possess any acquaintance whatever with education *as a science*, unless the substance of what has been written on the subject by practical men, can be placed before them at a cheap rate and in a small compass. Of the four hundred and sixty young persons who, during the period to which I have already referred, have left our own institution to assume the responsible office of instructors, I know very few to whom a volume of this character, however imperfectly executed, would not have been, at their first setting out, a treasure.

3. The great defect in most books of education, it has been well observed by an experienced teacher, is, that " we are taught almost exclusively how to operate on the *individual*. It is the error into which theoretic writers almost always fall. We are

continually meeting with remarks which sound very well by the fire-side, but which are totally inefficient and useless in school, from their being apparently based upon the supposition, that the teacher has but *one* pupil to attend to at a time. The great question, however, in the management of *schools*, is, not how you can take one scholar, and lead him forward most rapidly in a prescribed course, but how you can classify and arrange *numbers*, comprising every possible variety, both as to knowledge and capacity, so as to carry them all forward effectually together. The whole business of public instruction, if it goes on at all, must go on by the teacher's skill in multiplying his power by acting on *numbers at once.*"* In selecting materials for my present undertaking, I have endeavoured constantly to keep the *spirit* of these remarks in mind.

4. While, however, I have been anxious to make the book thoroughly *practical*, and in this respect as useful as possible to those who are employed in the daily instruction of the children of the poor, I have not forgotten the importance of directing attention to *principles*, capable of a diversified application, rather than to methods or exercises, which, however excellent in themselves, may be, to a great extent, inseparable from a particular system. Teachers in general would, I know, much rather be told of some definite way by which they may push

---

* The Teacher, by Jacob Abbott, chap. iii.

forward their pupils, than be led to principles which, applied *in almost any way*, would insure advantageous results. But this indolent habit of mind should by no means be encouraged; a teacher who would excel, must *reflect:* the mechanical adoption of plans, without reference to the principles on which they rest, is unworthy of an intelligent and manly mind.

5. The *order* which I have followed in introducing the various topics necessarily brought under notice, is that which appeared to me most natural; and, on the whole, best adapted to furnish a clear and condensed view of the entire subject. Under each head will be found, I may venture to say, many practical remarks of great value, the suggestions of experienced teachers either in this country, in Germany, or in the United States of America. It would have afforded me much pleasure to have given the *name* of every writer whose sentiments have been thus transferred to the present volume, but this act of justice I have found myself unable to perform. One source, however, from which I have drawn unsparingly, must be specially mentioned. I refer to the " American Annals of Education and Instruction," edited by the Rev. W. C. Woodbridge, of Boston, U. S., a journal of which it is impossible for me to speak too highly; I scarcely know the extent of my obligations to this educational treasury. Still, with all the aid I have been able to obtain, my task has been sufficiently

arduous. It would have been easy to *write* a volume on education, and still easier to compile one: to collate the views of nearly seventy different authors, and to *express* (if I may borrow a chemical phrase) the result of their investigations, I have found both difficult and laborious, but in no other way could the *kind* of book that is wanted be produced.

6. How far the main object of the undertaking, the preparation of a suitable *text-book* for young teachers, has been attained, remains to be seen; an approximation to what is desired, is perhaps all that, under the circumstances, can reasonably be expected. In the absence of any thing better, however, this may have its use; and hence, to facilitate examination on its contents, either orally or by means of written compositions, a series of questions adapted to bring out the most important points has been added, and each paragraph numbered; an arrangement which has this additional advantage, that it permits an easy reference to past observations, in cases where it would otherwise be necessary to indulge in repetition.

7. Some *incidental* benefits may, I trust also not unreasonably, be expected to result from the publication of this little volume. It may serve to show those who desire the office of a teacher, either for themselves, or for a distressed dependent, that something beyond the mere *wish* to do good, is necessary in order to effect good; that one chief

reason why schools are not more useful will be found in the fact, that instructors have not qualified themselves for usefulness; and that it is utterly vain to expect lessons of virtue and wisdom, from men who flee to the preceptor's chair only as a refuge from destitution,—*the last hope of the unfortunate.*

8. Another, and not less important end will be attained, if the book should lead in any quarter even to *an attempt* to purify the sources of moral influence in schools. The very endeavour, whether successful or not, would do good. It is mortifying to think, that amid all the diversified enterprises of Christian benevolence, no combined effort should yet have been made, to develop and secure the vast amount of moral and spiritual energy which is now every day trodden down in our elementary schools by the foot of ignorance; or, which is worse, perverted by a wicked ingenuity to bad purposes: —that a field which (not less for its extent, than for the abundant harvest which it promises to the cultivator,) claims to rank second in importance to none beside, should, as if by common consent, remain unoccupied; or be abandoned to the blunders of the incompetent, and the speculations of the empiric. When this crying evil shall be remedied, and not before, will faithful and well-instructed teachers be either diligently sought for, or justly remunerated. Happy indeed, should I be, if anything I could say or do, might tend to promote the comfort, or enhance in public estimation the value of a

class of men, whose services are yet but little understood, and whose thankless and ill-paid office is a standing and bitter satire upon an age, in many other respects justly termed liberal and enlightened.

9. Much of the present volume must of necessity be found inapplicable to the conduct and general management of *Sunday schools;* yet to the *Teachers* of these important institutions some of the hints may notwithstanding be valuable. Education is not less a science, nor is teaching less an art, because the exclusive subject of instruction is moral and religious truth; the instrument in every case is the same; and the general laws by which that instrument may be best fitted to discover and to apply truth, are one and identical. All questions, therefore, relating either to the nature or management of mind, or to the practical application of those laws by which mind is to be governed or strengthened, cannot fail to be interesting to the intelligent Sunday school teacher. Besides, we must never forget, that Sunday schools are the legitimate and fruitful nurseries of our best day school teachers. There, if any where, shall we find the self-denial, the patience, the perseverance, and the piety, without which all other accomplishments are utterly useless in a school for the poor; and hence it becomes of the highest importance, that the friends of day school instruction should leave no means untried to render Sunday school teachers

thoroughly acquainted with the *principles* of education; and, if possible, deeply to imbue them with a spirit of intelligent inquiry on all subjects bearing directly or indirectly upon their sacred employment.

10. To Missionaries, and others, who are engaged in the establishment of schools in foreign lands, this book will, I trust, not be unacceptable. How many of them have again and again written to me, lamenting bitterly their want of information on the best modes of educating the young! How many have said to me, "We do not so much want the detail of mechanical arrangements,—these we can obtain from existing publications,—as *general principles* of government and of instruction, which will admit of application under varying circumstances, and which are capable of being carried out, in other states of society than that in which it is your privilege to live." Of what use is a brief and official letter in reply to inquiries like these? The men want illustrations, examples,—a hundred things which a letter can never contain. In future, while I shall still deeply regret that I have not other and better books to send them, I shall have the satisfaction of offering them this small proof of my sympathy with their difficulties, and of my *desire* at least to aid in their removal.

11. Still, the main object of the work is the improvement of our *home* schools, and the elevation of our *English* elementary teachers. Until this is

effected, a deadly apathy will continue to chill every effort to extend education, and cold contempt still wither the aspirations of those, who, but for this burden, would cheerfully devote themselves to the arduous and important duties of the school. " I have been the tutor of princes," said the friend of Silvio Pellico, " I am now ambitious to *rise* to the elevation of a schoolmaster to the poor."* If that noble sentiment found a cordial response in British bosoms, I should say of England, " the day of her deliverance draweth nigh." But it does *not* meet with such response, and it never will, until the moral power which yet slumbers in our schools, is, in far greater degree than heretofore, recognised, developed, and sanctified. *The improvement of education will alone lead to its extension.* Then, and not till then, will the benevolent anticipations of one of nature's sweetest poets find their happy fulfilment, and mankind witness

> —" The coming of that glorious time,
> When, prizing knowledge as her noblest wealth
> And best protection, this imperial realm,
> While she exacts allegiance, shall admit
> An obligation, on her part, to *teach*
> Them who are born to serve her and obey;
> Binding herself by statute, to secure
> For all the children whom her soil maintains,
> The rudiments of letters; and to inform
> The mind with moral and religious truth."†

---

* Speech of Henry Meyer, Esq. of Rome, at the meeting of the British and Foreign School Society.
† Wordsworth—" The Excursion."

LETTER II. TO A YOUNG TEACHER.

THE PLEASANTNESS OF TEACHING.

12. " Most persons," says Sir Walter Scott, " must have witnessed with delight, the joyous burst which attends the dismissing of a village school on a fine summer evening. The buoyant spirit of childhood, repressed with so much difficulty during the tedious hours of discipline, may then be seen to explode, as it were, in shout, and song, and frolic, as the little urchins join in groups on their playground, and arrange their matches of sport for the evening. But there is one individual who partakes of the relief afforded by the moment of dismission, whose feelings are not so obvious to the eye of the spectator, or so apt to receive his sympathy. I mean the teacher himself, who, stunned with the hum, and suffocated with the closeness of his schoolroom, has spent the whole day (himself against a host) in controlling petulance, exciting indifference to action, striving to enlighten stupidity, and labouring to soften obstinacy; and whose very powers of intellect have been confounded by hearing the same dull lesson repeated a hundred times by rote,

and only varied by the various blunders of the reciters. If to these mental distresses are added a delicate frame of body, and a mind ambitious of some higher distinction than that of being the tyrant of childhood, the reader may have some slight conception of the relief which a solitary walk in the cool of a fine summer evening affords to the head which has ached, and the nerves which have been shattered, for so many hours, in plying the irksome task of public instruction."

13. What a picture! The " tyrant of childhood," making his escape from the dulness and noise, the heat and suffocation, the tears and punishment of his wretched empire! Who, with such a prospect before him, would be a school-master? If this touching and graphic description, so true to nature, must be realised by the teacher, what strange mockery to speak of *the pleasantness of teaching!* Happily for our purpose, however, it *need* not be realised; the tyranny and tears, the dulness and the distraction, may all be dispensed with; and enjoyments of the highest and purest kind, mutually shared by the teacher and the taught, be made to occupy their places. It *is* thus with some, and therefore it *may* be thus, with you, and with all. The fact is, there are *conditions* of happiness in a school, as well as in every other situation in life; and if these conditions be not observed, neither peace nor comfort can be found within its precincts. Permit me to enumerate some of them.

14. The first is, ABILITY TO GOVERN BY MORAL MEANS. In a school it is of course necessary to *resolve to rule;* but this is not *all* that is necessary. Children are, to a much greater extent than is generally supposed, reasonable and intelligent beings; they are just as much influenced by *motives* as adults; and they must be governed very much in the same way. Now, if a teacher, disregarding this obvious truth, insists upon ruling simply by the exercise of blind and brute force, he must expect to reap the reward of his folly in the uneasiness, vexation, and perplexity which such a course will inevitably bring upon him. Nor is this all. By so doing, he at once chokes up the spring of some of the highest enjoyments of which the human mind is susceptible. All men love power, especially *moral power.* The exercise of this kind of power, or what we call *influence,* is universally grateful; the intensity, the exquisiteness of the enjoyment depending upon the number of minds which can be influenced; the perfection or dominant character of the influence itself; and the difficulties which have been surmounted,—the skill that has been exercised,—the amount of *mind* which has been brought to bear, in its attainment. "It is this," says Mr. Abbott, " which gives interest to the plans and operations of human governments. They can do little by actual force. Nearly all the power that is held even by the most despotic executive, must be based on an adroit management of the principles of human

nature, so as to lead men voluntarily to co-operate with the ruler in his plans." Now this particular kind of gratification, the able teacher enjoys in the highest perfection. His school is the field of his enterprise: in proportion to his skill and ingenuity in managing human nature, is the extent of his success; and in that success he finds an immediate and rich reward. To lead, simply by the power of his own mind, a hundred other minds in willing captivity; to turn the very waywardness and restlessness of childhood to the accomplishment of his own matured plans and purposes; and to do all this, without crushing the buoyancy of one spirit, or checking the flow of natural gladness in any one heart, is a triumph and a joy, abundantly compensating the toil and care by which it has been effected. These few remarks will sufficiently explain what I understand by the ability to govern by moral means. The whole subject of government will come under notice in my next letter.

15. The second condition of happiness in a school is BENEVOLENCE. That was a beautiful saying of Dr. Dwight, "*He that makes a little child happier for half an hour is a co-worker with God.*" It precisely expresses the spirit which pervades the bosom of a happy teacher. I have sometimes observed the working of this heavenly principle under circumstances of great outward discouragement. One wonders that a man should remain where there is so little to cheer him. The reason is obvious.

He loves his work just because he delights in the exercise of the benevolent affections. His schoolroom is a happy place, because it is the theatre of his good-will,—the place where his kindest and best feelings are developed and exercised. He has emotions there into which " a stranger cannot enter." His relationship to *it*, is distinct from that which belongs to any other locality. It is his own exclusive domain,—the territory within which his influence is paramount. There, every individual is his distinct charge; and as he seeks to stamp upon each the impress of his own mind and character, he finds his reward in that peculiar blessedness which, by the very constitution of human nature, invariably attends the humblest effort to benefit another.

16. A third condition of happiness, is UNFLINCHING FAITH IN THE EFFICACY OF EARLY INSTRUCTION AS A MEANS OF MORAL REGENERATION. On this point there should be no misgivings. Whatever others may think, the teacher must be satisfied, that any great moral change in the community, will be *mainly* effected by the instrumentality of schools; that this is God's *appointed* way of spreading sacred and salutary influences throughout the whole community. I have known some teachers singularly deficient in this essential characteristic of a good instructor. Instead of rejoicing in the hopes and expectations which attach by eminence to *their* ministry, you see plainly enough they altogether distrust it. The seed does not spring up imme-

diately, and they at once conclude that it is all choked by the thorns. Because another and distinct agency is employed by God to gather in the harvest, from that which is employed to plough and to sow, they attach *efficiency* only to the latter, and forget the promise that " he who soweth and they who reap shall one day *rejoice together.*" Now this temper of mind is as unphilosophic as it is unscriptural. Reflect, I pray you, on the peculiar facilities which are afforded by your particular position, not only for doing good, but for doing it most extensively! Is it no advantage to turn up the yet unbroken soil, and to sow the *first* seeds? Is it nothing, to hold in your hand a chain of communication, linking *your* mind, not merely with a hundred other minds, but with all the minds that through all time shall ever be influenced by those who received their earliest impressions from you? Is it no special honour to be the servant of the feeblest, the most inexperienced and the most helpless?—to stand at the portico, as it were, of the temple of God, keeping the house, and guarding it from pollution? And is all this arrangement of Providence subservient to no end? Is it productive of no good result? If you have brought yourself to believe this, depend upon it, my friend, the error has more to do with the heart than with the head. There is but one *radical* cure for this distemper of the mind, and that is, calm and prayerful meditation on the word, the ways, and the promises of

God. Bring your weariness and distrust " to the light," and, it cannot fail " to be reproved." So long as it is cherished and indulged, it is impossible that you can be happy in your work.

17. Subordinate, indeed, to these essential elements of happiness, yet still materially affecting the degree of comfort which a teacher will enjoy in his school, are two other qualifications, which may just be hinted at. The first is, the ABILITY TO INTEREST children; not only to make them happy, but happy *in the performance of duty*; a capability which mainly depends on the attention paid by a teacher, to what the Germans call " *didaktik*," or the art of communicating instruction: but as this will form the subject of a distinct letter, it need not now be further adverted to. The second is, COMPETENT INFORMATION; by which I mean, not merely the possession of just sufficient knowledge to conduct the school, but, such a complete and *accurate* acquaintance on the part of the teacher, with the *elements* of that which he has to teach, as shall give him the perfect mastery of all its parts, and unlimited confidence in the correctness of his instructions. Any branch of science which is not *thus* known, is not our own; it must be ranked among the lands that are yet to be possessed. No man can clearly and simply *explain* to a child, any thing with which he is not himself perfectly acquainted. To *illustrate* successfully much more is necessary; a considerable share of information on many sub-

jects is essential to success in this department. A good teacher knows and feels this, and since all knowledge is congruous, he is always on the *look out* for materials of instruction. It is thus he learns his own ignorance. The further he advances, the more he finds how necessary it is, that *he who undertakes to teach others, should take time to prepare himself.*

18. Still, in order to be successful as a teacher, it is not necessary to be proficient in every thing, nor is it either wise or honest to make any such pretensions. A man brings a great deal of unnecessary anxiety, irritation, and consequent misery upon himself, when he is afraid to confess ignorance. "I remember well (says professor Jardine) the striking effect produced on the minds of the students, by an instance of great simplicity and candour, on the part of the late venerable Dr. Reid, when he was professor of moral philosophy in this university (Glasgow). During the hour of examination they were reading to him a portion of Cicero de Finibus; when at one of those mutilated and involved passages which occasionally occur in that work, the student who was reading stopped, and was unable to proceed. The doctor attempted to explain the difficulty; but the meaning of the sentence did not immediately present itself. Instead, however, of slurring it over, as many would have done, "Gentlemen," said he, "I thought I had the meaning of this passage, but it has escaped

me; I shall, therefore, be obliged to any one of you who will translate it." A student thereupon instantly stood up in his place, and translated it to the doctor's satisfaction. He politely thanked him for it, and farther commended the young man for his spirited attempt. This incident had a powerful effect upon the minds of the other students, while all admired the candour of that eminent professor; nor was there a single difficult passage, which was not afterwards studied with more than usual care, that the next precious opportunity for distinction might be seized." Act in this spirit, and you will lose nothing by renouncing all claim to infallibility.

19. The interest which strangers will take in visiting your school,—the notion *they* will have of the pleasantness of teaching, (and this is a matter of no trifling importance,) will depend very much upon your skill in exhibiting that which is most likely to be generally interesting to your visitors. You ought not to complain of the inattention and indifference of influential persons in your neighbourhood, if you take no pains to interest them. Only ensure good order; a clean and well-ventilated school-room; and happy faces; and human nature must be strangely changed, if you do not find your full share of persons anxious to witness your intelligent and well-directed experiments on the youthful mind. After all, however, you must not expect that strangers will ever properly estimate the value and efficiency of your labours. They *can*

only do so, when they know what the children were at the time of their entrance. That some, who know well the mass of pollution from which many of these poor children have been "excavated," should display so little interest in the character of their day-school instruction, is, I confess, surprising and perplexing. Neither day schools nor Sunday schools have yet that hold on the affections of the church which they deserve. I am informed that a few years ago, in the United States, the Governors of New Jersey and Connecticut, three of the judges of Pennsylvania, and ten or twelve of their most distinguished lawyers, were *Sunday school teachers.* This is as it should be. " If this world is to become a better and a happier world, not our Sunday schools merely, but all our schools, from the infant school to the university, must be under the superintendence of the *best and wisest* of the community."*

20. One other observation will conclude this letter. *No man can be happy as a teacher, who is not prepared to devote all his powers to the performance of its duties.* Fellenberg does not ask too much, in demanding for this office, " a vigilance that never sleeps, a perseverance that never tires." Nothing short of this will suffice. How strange then is the delusion of those who rush towards it, as the elysium of indolence! That such should be unhappy in the employment, is a source of gratifi-

* Woodbridge.

cation rather than of regret. Let them flee to some other occupation, for here they will find no resting place for the soles of their feet. The motto of Luther, "Work on earth, and rest in heaven," must be the motto of every faithful schoolmaster; and he who is not prepared to live and act in this spirit, had better leave the service to warmer hearts and nobler minds. Such a man will never know anything of the elevated delights which associate themselves with the employment; he may have the drudgery, but he will not find the pleasures of the exercise; he belongs to that class, of whom Fenelon beautifully says, in relation to another (and yet not another) service, "They perceive what it deprives them of, but they do not see what it bestows; they exaggerate its sacrifices, without looking at its consolations." How can such as these know anything of *the pleasantness of teaching?*

LETTER III.   TO THE SAME.

GOVERNMENT OF A SCHOOL.

21. "That lad," said Dr. Johnson, when speaking of a sullen and unhappy boy, "looks like the son of a schoolmaster;" which, added he, "is one of the very worst conditions of childhood. Such a boy has no father, or worse than none; he never can reflect on his parent, but the reflection brings to his mind some idea of pain inflicted, or of sorrow suffered." Can we wonder that an office, which, in the eye even of the great moralist, (himself a teacher,) was thus associated with every thing that is hateful and degrading, should, by almost common consent, be looked upon with a feeling bordering on contempt?

22. I have already observed (14) that children must be governed to a great extent in the same way as men are, viz. by the adaptation of plans to the fixed and uniform tendencies of human nature. At the same time, it is fully allowed, that the government of a school is necessarily *arbitrary* in its character; it must be power, exercised by the

will of one man, according to circumstances of which he alone is the judge. Now there are two ways, and but two ways, of obtaining power of this description,—one is by *force*, the other, by *influence*. Both are necessary in their places, according to the age and character of those who are the subjects of discipline; but both are not equally suitable for the school. An infant cannot be reasoned with, and therefore Locke was right in commending the mother who whipped her baby eight times before she subdued it; for had she stopped at the seventh act of correction, her daughter would have been ruined.*
But a child of eight or ten years of age is a *reasonable* being; and therefore Dr. Johnson was wrong in arguing, in defence of Hastie, that school boys "can be governed only by fear; that no stated rules can ascertain the degrees of scholastic, more than of military punishment, but that it must be enforced till it overpowers temptation, till stubbornness becomes flexible and perverseness regular." Lord Mansfield, in his judgment on the same case, which he pronounced in the House of Lords,

---

* Dr. Bryce thinks, that in very early infancy, pain has a moral as well as a physical effect,—the effect which a blister has on the body, producing what is medically termed counter irritation. Thus the child's attention is withdrawn by the present pain from the fretfulness which made it unhappy, its happiness is restored, and good is done by the withdrawing of its mind from a bad object. In well-regulated infant schools, however, very young children are governed without any corporal punishment.

showed himself both a wiser and a better man, when he exclaimed, " My Lords, *severity* is not the way to govern either boys or men."*

23. Let us then try to find out " a more excellent way." Putting aside, therefore, the old notion of *brute force*, as unfit to be applied for the purposes of government, when the reasoning powers are possessed and developed, let us see how moral means, or what we term *influence*, may be brought to bear in this service.

24. The first thing to be attended to in every school is GOOD ORDER. This point, not less essential to the comfort of the teacher, and to the communication of instruction, than it is to the happiness and the moral welfare of the child, must be gained at all hazards. The want of order is the great master defect of nearly all schools. I know of no one thing which so powerfully counteracts the exertions of teachers as this want of good discipline.† It is a great mistake to attend to instruction as the *first* thing; the love of order, punctuality,

---

* Dr. Johnson's argument in this case, may be found at length in the Appendix to Boswell's Johnson, vol. iii. Murray's edition.

† It will be seen that I use this word here, and I shall do so in future, in its modern and limited sense, as referring to control; and not in its more legitimate and extended signification, as relating to the whole course of instruction. I make this remark because Professor Pillans, in his very useful " Letters on Elementary Teaching," adopts the latter sense, as corresponding to *disciplina,* in the writings of Cicero and Quintilian.

and cleanliness, ought to be awakened *before* the means of knowledge are increased; and this, not because literary instruction is less important, but because discipline is itself a principal means both of moral and intellectual improvement. Every intelligent being sees and feels the beauty of order when he finds himself surrounded by it, and children do so even more than adults. A good teacher will know how to turn this *natural taste* for arrangement to account. I will only add that, whatever may in other respects be the talents of an instructor, if he cannot maintain good order, he is worse than useless as a moral governor of the young; he takes rank with the incompetent and the indolent.

25. The question then arises, How is order to be obtained? I should reply, by letting it be understood from the first that you are *determined* to have it. Good or bad arrangements,—a well or ill-chosen system, (matters with which your pupils have nothing to do,) will, of course, materially affect the *degree* of order which can be maintained, and will also make a wide difference in the ease or difficulty of obtaining it. I am not now, however, speaking of systems, but of the kind of influence which must be exercised in order to make *any* system work quietly, regularly, and efficiently. And here nothing can be done without *unbending, inflexible determination* on the part of the teacher. He must be an absolute monarch, and he must speak and act as a man " having authority."

26. These last words start a new train of thought. They suggest the idea of ONE, before whom, not the waywardness of childhood, but the wickedness of mature and hardened malignity, cowed and was abashed; and yet He was " meek and lowly," a " man of sorrows," in rank a servant, and in temper a lamb. With this example before us, need I add, that the voice and look of authority are quite compatible with a spirit of gentleness, love, and true humility? Ah! you will say, but HE was " the Holy One!" True! that was the secret of his power. While he commanded others he was himself governed; not indeed by men, but by *principles*; and so must you too, if, like him, you would be in your appropriate place, the object at once of fear and of love. LAW (not caprice) must rule in your school; law, of which Hooker beautifully says, " Her seat is the bosom of God, her voice the harmony of the world; all things in heaven and earth do her homage, the very least as feeling her care, and the very greatest as not exempted from her power; both angels and men, and creatures of what condition soever, though each in different sort and manner, yet all with uniform consent, admiring her as the mother of their peace and joy." But this is digression.

27. In enforcing authority, especially over numbers, *attention must be paid to the tones of the voice.* A horse, it has been shrewdly observed, soon perceives the timidity of his rider by the

shaking of his legs, and no sooner does he suspect fear than he refuses to obey. Children, in like manner, instinctively discover by the tones of the voice when a teacher is unable to enforce obedience; and the moment that discovery is made, his power is gone. He may implore, or he may be imperious; he will only excite their scorn. You will see that what I refer to, has little to do with what is termed a good or bad voice; it is not a question of high or low notes, and still less of loudness and vociferation. It is only *as an index to the mind*, as indicating the determination within, that the tones of the voice become important; and this kind of demonstration you will at once perceive, may be conveyed as well in a whisper as in a shout. Only let it be a *living* voice, expressing the calm and quiet determination of a mind conscious of its strength, and it will rarely be resisted.

28. Bear in mind then, that the first step you have to take, in moral, as well as in intellectual education, is, to ESTABLISH YOUR AUTHORITY. There never was a more absurd notion than that which is becoming popular in some quarters, that children may be governed without authority, by moral suasion alone; that is to say, that they may be brought to love duty without any intervention of arbitrary command. Do not listen to this mischievous trash for a moment. To what *extent* it may be possible to substitute explanations and reasons for commands, I do not pretend to say; but

this I am sure of, no good will be done unless the child knows that *authority is at hand* if reason should fail; and let me add, I account that moral discipline little worth, which does not teach a child to submit to authority, *simply as authority.* "There are moments in the course of education, and even of life, when the delay which reasoning demands, would expose us to the danger which it is intended to avert, and where we must learn to yield to authority without a question."* Mr. Abbott, in a paper published in the American Annals of Education, illustrates this principle in his usual happy manner. He says, " Power is not useless because it lies dormant. The government of the United States employs its hundreds of workmen at Springfield, and at Harper's Ferry, in the manufacture of muskets. The inspector examines every one as it is finished, with great care. He adjusts the flint, and tries it again and again, until its emitted shower of sparks is of proper brilliancy; and when satisfied that all is right, he packs it away with its thousand companions, to sleep probably in their boxes in quiet obscurity for ever. A hundred thousand of these deadly instruments form a volcano of slumbering power which never has been awakened, and which we hope never will be. The government never makes use of them. One of its agents, a custom-house officer, waits upon you for the payment of a bond. He brings no musket. He keeps

---

* Woodbridge.

no troops. He comes with the gentleness and civility of a social visit. But you know, that if compliance with the just demands of your government is refused, and the resistance is sustained, force after force would be brought to bear upon you, until the whole hundred thousand muskets should speak with their united and tremendous energy. Such ought to be the character of all government. The teacher of a school, especially, must act upon these principles. He will be mild and gentle in his manners; in his intercourse with his pupils he will use the language and assume the air, not of stern authority, but of request and persuasion. But there must be authority at the bottom to sustain him, or he can do nothing successfully, especially in attempting to reach the hearts of his pupils. The reason why it is necessary is this. First, the man who has not the full, unqualified, complete control of his scholars, must spend his time and wear out his spirits in preserving any tolerable order in his dominions; and, secondly, he who has not authority will be so constantly vexed and fretted by the occurrences which will take place around him, that all his moral power will be neutralized by the withering influence of his clouded brow. To do good to our pupils, our own spirits must be composed and at rest; and especially, if we wish to influence favourably the hearts of others, our own must rise above the troubled waters of irritation and anxious care."

29. Authority once established, obedience will be

prompt, and very soon become habitual. No obedience, indeed, is worth the name, which is not prompt, habitual, and, I might add, cheerful. A languid and dilatory yielding to repeated commands is rank disobedience. "Not as in my presence only, but also in my absence," must be the requirement; and nothing short of this is worthy of commendation. *I know that it is attainable.* I have again and again seen a school of five hundred boys proceeding for a whole day, with the most perfect order and regularity, in the absence of every *adult* person capable of exercising even a shadow of authority. The moral influence of the absent teacher, aided only by subordinate arrangements among the boys, was governing hundreds who would have gloried in defying any exhibition of mere force.

30. But it is not enough to *assert* for a time, even successfully, your claim to unqualified submission; authority must be maintained through a long course of years, under every diversity of circumstance, and with a constant succession of new scholars. Now this cannot be done by the mere exercise of WILL, however strong that will may be. You must now, therefore, endeavour to ascertain by what means you can gain *an habitual ascendancy* over the minds of the young. Every one must have noticed the different degrees of influence exerted by different individuals in the same circumstances. "Take," says Mr. Hall, "as an example, the case of two ministers of the Gospel, on the whole

similarly circumstanced with regard to their congregations; the one almost idolized, the other barely treated with respect. What occasions the difference? The office is the same, and human nature is the same. The difference is in the men; and it consists, probably, rather in their respective tempers and dispositions, than in any inequality of talent or attainments. It is precisely thus in schools. In some schools, every word which proceeds from the mouth of the master is eagerly seized upon and attended to; in others, it is as habitually disregarded."* I shall now just enumerate some directions in relation to this subject which have been suggested to me by the remarks of practical men.

31. First,—*Endeavour to convince your scholars that you are their friend,*—that you aim at their improvement, and desire their good. It will not take long to satisfy them of this, if you *are* so in reality. Remember, however, that a mere declaration of being their friend will be very far from proving you to be such, or convincing them of it. You must prove it to them, by showing a greater regard for their welfare than for your own ease. In brief, LOVE them, and that will go a long way towards governing them.

---

* Vide Hall's Lectures to Schoolmasters, Boston, 1833; a work of considerable value, and which has met with a large circulation in the United States. — See also Salzmann, Abbott, &c.

32. Secondly,—*Never give a command which you are not resolved to see obeyed.* To give commands which you have not time, or ability, or perhaps intention, to enforce, is to inculcate disobedience. If, therefore, you make a promise, keep it. If you say that neglect of duty shall be followed by punishment, be sure to inflict it. If you require a child to do this or that, see that it is done exactly as you require it. By keeping this important principle in mind, you will take care not to be *hasty* either in commanding or threatening. Deliberation is always important to any man who has to exercise authority over a community. Take care, however, not to confound this wise delay with dilatoriness. Promptitude is the soul of discipline, when you have to deal with numbers: he who is thinking *what* he should do, and *how* he should do it, when the time for action is come, is sure to be vanquished.

33. Thirdly,—*Try to create throughout the school a popular sentiment in favour of order and virtue.* It is well known by those who are acquainted with collective bodies of the young, that it is next to impossible to carry into effect for any length of time a regulation, however important, which is opposed to PUBLIC OPINION. Every school, however humble, has an atmosphere of its own; there are certain prevalent notions which give a decided and *peculiar* character to the whole community. Now these sentiments and notions will generally be regulated by a very limited number of the pupils,

the master spirits of their little world; and it depends very much on the conduct of the teacher, whether these young demagogues shall be as thorns in his side, or whether they shall become the very pillars of his strength. These boys will probably be found among the most unruly and the most mischievous. The natural energy of their characters; the elasticity of their spirits; their consciousness of vigour; will all tend to make them troublesome subjects. It is the more important therefore, that a teacher should secure the *co-operation* of such characters in his plans; that he should find out a way to their hearts, and that he should know how to turn all this activity of mind into a channel of his own digging. Fellenberg appears to have accomplished much in this way. " The effort is constant to excite in the pupils that public spirit which seeks to exclude every thing improper from its sphere of influence, in order to preserve the order and tranquillity which are necessary to the improvement of all. In the same manner the attempt is made to inspire a class with a desire to attain the object proposed in their lessons, and a spirit of opposition to all that disorder and idleness which may interrupt or embarrass the course of instruction, or retard their progress. An influence of this kind, once established, with due regulation and oversight, will often accomplish more than all the remonstrances and discipline of the teacher. The pupil can seldom resist the force of truth when he finds himself condemned by the common voice of his companions, and is often more humbled by this censure from his equals, than by any of the admonitions of his superiors."*

34. In making these observations, however, you must not suppose that I am at all advocating a plan which has been tried in some schools, viz., the embodying of this corrected public sentiment in a code of regulations to be administered by the pupils themselves. On the contrary, I quite disapprove of all such attempts to make children govern themselves, as injurious to the cultivation of a proper spirit of subordination to elders; as consuming, and I think wasting, a great deal of valuable time; and, especially, as destructive of that private and friendly admonition which in well-regulated youthful society is more frequently *understood* than expressed. Besides all this, cases are continually arising where a mature judgment is needed to distinguish properly the amount of guilt that has been incurred.

35. To gain the kind of ascendancy you wish, however, over what I have before called the master spirits of the school, you must know how to secure the confidence and affection of *all*. You cannot, it is true, act the parent, to one, or, it may be, two hundred children; you cannot become acquainted with every trait of character which may distinguish

---

* Sketches of Hofwyl, by the Rev. W. C. Woodbridge.

each; you cannot follow them into the street or the field, and detect the motives which influence, and the feelings which are predominant, when they are away from your eye, and no longer under your control; but you can do much to secure such a share of their cordial attachment and esteem, as shall materially influence their conduct wherever they may be, or whatever may be their pursuits.

36. Do you ask *how* this is to be done? I reply, in the first place,—*Observe in your conduct towards them* STRICT IMPARTIALITY. Children are eagle-eyed in the detection of injustice. That which is law, therefore, for one, must be law for all. It is true that you will, and must have, your *preferences;* and you *ought* to show that you exercise feelings towards those who are habitually diligent and obedient, very different from the sentiments you entertain towards the idle and perverse. This is *just*, and affords no reasonable ground of complaint. The wrong commences, when this preference is carried to the hall of legislation, and to the judgment seat; and when the uncouth and disagreeable are made to bear burdens for their transgressions, from which the amiable and more generous are in great measure exempt. Now, whatever be the motive, if you allow yourself to act thus unfairly, you will lose the *confidence* of your school.

37. Again, if you would win the hearts of the young, you must RESPECT THEIR FEELINGS. Children are very sensitive, and easily wounded to the

quick. A sneer, at what is sometimes termed by cold and worldly men, youthful enthusiasm, may do irreparable mischief. I once saw a child all but ruined for life in this way. The contemptuous sarcasm went to the inmost soul, and dried up in a moment of time the sweet waters of affection, as they rushed back with unnatural haste to the fountain from which they had just before issued, leaping with life and gladness. To many persons, I am aware, this species of sensibility is totally incomprehensible. It is an Egyptian hieroglyphic, which they cannot make out. There are others, however, who can read and understand it, and I trust you are among that number.

38. In connexion with this subject, *Be careful how you exercise the "power of rebuke."* Mr. Abbott carries this point so far as to insist upon the propriety of conveying reproof, not only privately, but *in writing*. In a large school this would be impracticable; but still something may be done in this way, and every teacher will find the advantage of acting, in the spirit at least, of the following admirable remarks. He says, " The more delicately you touch the feelings of your pupils, the more tender these feelings will become. Many a teacher hardens and stupifies the moral sense of his pupils, by the harsh and rough exposures to which he drags out the private feelings of the heart. A man may easily produce such a state of feeling in his school-room, that to address even the gentlest reproof to

any individual in the hearing of the next, would be a most severe punishment; and on the other hand, he may so destroy that sensitiveness, that his vociferated reproaches will be as unheeded as the wind. Besides, if a boy does something wrong, and you severely reprove him in the presence of his class, you punish the class almost as much as you do him. In fact, in many cases you punish them more; for I believe it is almost invariably more unpleasant for a good boy to stand by and listen to rebukes, than for a bad one to take them." *

39. Further, *Reproofs should always be administered in sorrow rather than in anger.* The more depraved the children with which you have to deal; the more they are accustomed at home to the voice of passion, or to the stroke of violence;—the greater the reprobate you are attempting to reform, the more needful is it to *adopt the language and tones of friendship* when obliged to rebuke. The susceptibility to love, as it is the first to be developed, so is it the last to be extinguished in the human bosom. Vice and profligacy, disease and misery, may have come in upon the soul like a flood; still it holds true, " many waters cannot quench love." Let this therefore always be your strong-hold.

40. The *Judicious use of Praise,* is another powerful means of gaining the affections of children. An encouraging smile, a gentle pressure of the

---

* The Teacher, p. 142 and 167. Seeley's edition.

hand, a word of commendation, will sometimes do wonders in the way of winning young hearts. Captain Basil Hall thus describes the effects produced on board ship by the different modes of government adopted by two different commanders. He says, "Whenever one of these officers came on board the ship, his constant habit was to cast his eye about him, in order to discover what was wrong; to detect the smallest thing that was out of its place; in a word, to find as many grounds for censure as possible. This constituted, in his opinion, the best preventive to neglect on the part of those under his command; and he acted in this severe way *on principle*. The attention of the other officer, on the contrary, appeared to be directed chiefly to those points which he could approve of. One of these captains would remark to the first lieutenant, as he walked along, "How white and clean you have got the decks to-day! I think you must have been at them all the morning, to have got them into such order." The other, in similar circumstances, but eager to find fault, would say, even if the decks were as white and clean as drifted snow, "I wish, sir, you would teach these sweepers to clear away that bundle of shakings!" pointing to a bit of rope yarn, not half an inch long, left under the truck of a gun. It seemed, in short, as if nothing was more vexatious to one of these officers than to discover things so correct as to afford him no good opportunity for finding fault; while, to the other, the necessity of censuring really appeared a punishment to himself. Under the one, accordingly, we all worked with cheerfulness, from a conviction that nothing we did in a proper way would miss approbation. But our duty under the other being performed in fear, seldom went on with much spirit. We had no personal satisfaction in doing things correctly, from the certainty of getting no commendation. What seemed the oddest thing of all was, that these men were both as kind-hearted as could be, or if there were any difference, the fault-finder was the better natured, and in matters not professional the more indulgent of the two." Captain Hall adds, " It requires but very little experience of soldiers or sailors, children, servants, or any other kind of dependents, to show that this good humour on our part towards those whom we wish to influence, is the best possible coadjutor to our schemes of management, whatever these may be."

41. Now, I do think, that if you avoid these three errors,—partiality, disregard to the feelings of the young, and a spirit of fault-finding,—it will not be difficult to secure a favourable reception in the school for any thing you may propose. This point then being gained, select a few of the most influential boys, and put some peculiar responsibility upon them. Since they *will* be leaders, *pre-occupy* their talent for command, and employ it on the side of order and industry. Trust them implicitly; let them see that you repose confidence in their

integrity and sense of honour, and you will rarely be disappointed. You will in this way frequently *create* the very virtue for the possession of which you give them credit; and they in turn, will in like manner act upon their fellows.

42. Fourthly. *Be uniform in your plans of government.* Be to-day what you were yesterday, and what you intend to be to-morrow. This is no easy matter, subject as all men are to variations in health and spirits, materially affecting the view they take of conduct. The manifest importance of uniformity will, however, suggest the necessity of taking every precaution not only against

> " those cataracts and breaks,
> Which humour interposed too often makes,"

but also against those little irregularities in the treatment of offences against discipline, which arise either from forgetfulness or caprice. To guard against this evil, first, *Have but few rules*, and see that these are well understood. Secondly, *Cultivate the habit of rigid self government.* Salzmann (an eminent teacher) goes so far as to insist that an instructor should always seek for the faults of his pupils in himself. He says, "If trouble arise in my school, I *examine myself*, and generally find that I am the cause of it—that either my body is out of order, or some unpleasant event has affected my spirits, or I am wearied out with excessive labour." Without, however, going this length, it should always be borne in mind, that children are eminently creatures of sympathy, and unconsciously assimilate themselves to those with whom they associate. Hence the importance of *habitual cheerfulness* on the part of the teacher, without which shadows and clouds will darken every brow.

43. Lastly, (to borrow a rule from Joseph Lancaster,) *Take care that every pupil shall at all times have something useful to do, and a motive for doing it.* In the neglect of all other rules, attention to this alone would secure, to a great extent, order and regularity. I need not suggest to you the peculiar facilities which are afforded by the monitorial system, for accomplishing this important object, as that subject will meet with distinct notice in another place. I would only observe, I do not see how it can be managed in a large school on any other plan.

44. In all that I have stated, however, remember, *The co-operation of the parents is to be sought*, and if possible, secured. They may be ignorant, or prejudiced, or capricious, or (which is more probable) they may be all these united; no matter, you must try to get them on your side. You must not disdain to reason with them on the importance of promoting the regular and early attendance of their children; you must send for, and advise with them, in cases where strong measures become necessary; and you must respect that strong and instinctive, though frequently blind, attachment to their young,

which may occasion them for a moment to resent as an injury, that which you inflicted only as a necessary duty. "It is an object with me," said one of our teachers to me, the other day, "to spend as much of my leisure time with the parents of the children as I possibly can. Until they *know* me, and in some degree respect me, I can of necessity exercise no influence over them. But when once this kind of acquaintance is formed, I can do *so* much, that to gain it I consider no sacrifice of time or trouble as too great." Still, they must not *govern* you; nor will they probably attempt it, if they find that while you are mild and courteous, you still know how to maintain your authority, and to carry out your plans with *unwavering firmness*.

45. The best mode of treating NEW SCHOLARS is often a perplexing consideration to young teachers; nor is it by any means an unimportant one. A child not unfrequently derives its strongest impressions with regard to school, from the events of the first few days or weeks after its admission. It is here then necessary to guard on the one hand, against an amount of indulgence which cannot be continued, and on the other, against a degree of strictness proper only to be exercised towards those who have been for some little time under the discipline of the school. Gentleness and decision combined, are essential; and nothing else will meet the irritation and insult to which a teacher is often exposed by new comers. Not a few *enter with a*

determination to have their own way, and the struggle which follows is always very trying to the temper of the instructor. These are the things that *test* his skill in the management of human nature, and according to his proficiency will be his success. In educating the ox for the plough, Mr. Cobbett very sensibly recommends that all violence and rough language should be avoided. " If he be stubborn, there should be no blows and no loud scolding. Stop; pat him; pat the other ox; and he will presently move on again. If he lie down, let him lie till he is tired; and when he chooses to get up treat him very gently, as if he had been doing every thing that was right. By these means a young ox will in a few days be broken to his labour. With gentle treatment, he is always of the same temper; always of the same aptitude to labour." A new scholar should be broken in, to the regulations of a school, if not in the same way, at least on the same principles.

46. But what is to be done with the thoroughly incorrigible; the one who has imbibed habits of confirmed depravity, and on whom admonitions and efforts have all been expended in vain? I think there can be but one answer—*dismiss him*. In this case there are bad influences *out of school*, operating more powerfully, and counteracting but too successfully the good influences of discipline and instruction. Unless these could be removed, the prospect of reformation is hopeless; and, therefore,

you are not only justified, but *bound*, out of regard to the welfare of the rest, at once to separate him from the school. In Sunday-schools, where it is possible to isolate in a great measure a youth of this description, and to keep him almost exclusively under the eye of a judicious teacher, it may be desirable to retain our hold as long as he is willing to attend, but in schools where numbers are to be governed by one teacher, this degree of care is manifestly impossible. It is then far better that one should be abandoned to his folly, than that the whole school should be corrupted by his iniquity.*

47. Before concluding this letter, I must very briefly refer to the too frequent absence of good order in Sunday-schools. I am not ignorant of the peculiar difficulties which stand in the way, and frequently impede the exercise of discipline in these institutions; difficulties arising out of the grand peculiarity, I should rather say distinguishing glory, of the Sunday-school system; and which are, I fear, inseparable from it. I refer to the *gratuitous* character of the agency employed. As a necessary consequence it is deficient in subordination, and marked by a natural jealousy of domination, which is highly injurious to good order. There is also in the minds of some Sunday-school teachers a constant shrinking from the exercise of authority, lest

* I have recently heard of two instances in which *expulsion* has led to the reformation of the offender. The possibility of this result should not be kept altogether out of sight.

the child should be disgusted with school, and withdraw itself altogether from the influences of christian instruction. The only remedy that I can suggest is, the adoption of a course which, I doubt not, has frequently been urged upon attention; viz. the exercise by teachers generally, of greater care in the selection of superintendents, and of greater humility in submitting to their arrangements. These men should be chosen chiefly on account of their ability to govern; and when chosen, they should be "esteemed very highly in love for their work's sake." From the remarks which have been made in this letter on the government of schools generally, many important *principles* may be gathered, which, with some trifling modifications, will admit of general adoption in Sunday-schools. The particular *mode* of their application must be left to the judgment of experienced teachers.

48. In conclusion, let me again remind you, that *children naturally love order*. They may not like the means by which alone it can be secured, but when it *is* secured, they are always the happier for it. A strict discipline, unstained by severity, never weaned the affections of any child, either from his school or his teacher. If, therefore, you would at once promote your own comfort, the happiness of your pupils, and their highest welfare—MAINTAIN GOOD GOVERNMENT.

LETTER IV. TO THE SAME.

THE MONITORIAL SYSTEM.

49. The most *obvious* advantage which the monitorial plan possesses over all others, is, without doubt, the greater facility which it affords for the maintenance of order and good government, by securing at all times the regular and constant employment of every pupil. It is equally evident that *the amount of knowledge* imparted in a school where the pupils are constantly occupied, will be very much greater than it can be in one where, every thing having to be managed by the teacher, aided perhaps only by a single individual, a large proportion of the children must, during many hours of the day, be comparatively idle.

50. But this is by no means the extent of benefit which may fairly be claimed on its behalf. Monitors are in some respects better teachers than adults; they sympathise more readily with the difficulties of the pupil; they are more patient in imparting knowledge, and more fertile in expedients for explaining

and illustrating it :* they communicate with more facility ; and, *learning while they teach*,† they will-

* Father Girard, the benevolent founder of the system of mutual instruction in Switzerland, told Mr. Woodbridge, when examining his school, that when he met with difficulty in explaining any word or subject to a child, he had often called in a boy more advanced, to aid him, and had usually found him succeed entirely, even when all his own efforts had failed. Mr. Wood (of Edinburgh) relates the following fact. " A learned mathematician," he tells us, " came to the Sessional School, for the purpose of exhibiting what he suggested as an improvement in the practice of one of the rules of arithmetic." It was necessary to explain the plan five times over, both to Mr. Wood, and to one of his best monitors, before either of them could understand it; but " the boy on his return to the school-room, so distinctly explained to one of his fellow monitors the method, that from this explanation *once* given, he, though much inferior to the first, was able to perform the operation." Professor Pillans bears similar testimony : he says, " Monitors are aware of the difficulties which they themselves encountered but lately, and are often able to explain them to their comrades, in a manner more familiar and intelligible than can be done by the master, whose habits and ways of thinking are so widely different." The experience of the central school in the Borough Road is precisely of the same character.

† " A monitor always improves *himself* as much as he does his pupils."—*Wood* and *Pillans*.

" Dr. Johnson used always to urge the importance of children being encouraged to *tell* whatever they hear particularly striking, to some brother, sister, or servant, before the impression was erased by the intervention of newer occurrences. His mother it seems was accustomed, when she had told him anything which she thought likely to seize his attention, to

ingly undertake an amount of labour, which would be to an adult intolerable drudgery. As *subordinate* instructors they are *far superior* to adults, inasmuch as, having no views of their own beyond the immediate accomplishment of the work to which they are appointed, they readily fall in with all the plans and directions of the superintending mind; and thus promote that unity of system and of action, which is so essential to success. The *intermediate position* they occupy, between the teacher and the scholars, enables them greatly to benefit both parties. Exempted from the weariness and disgust consequent upon incessant attempts to communicate the more mechanical branches of learning, the teacher is able to direct a large share of his attention to the advancement of the elder scholars; while the children, delivered from the irksome listlessness attendant upon the old methods of instruction, instead of forming habits of inattention and idleness, the miserable influence of which may cling to them through life,—or expending their natural energies in every form of annoyance and of mischief,—are unitedly and agreeably engaged, in advancing their own improvement,—in promoting

---

send him to a favourite workman in the house, to whom she knew he would communicate the conversation while it was yet impressed on his mind. The event was what she wished; and *it was to that method chiefly that he owed his uncommon felicity of remembering distant occurrences.—Piozzi.*

the happiness of their teacher,—and in securing the well-being of their fellow scholars.

51. The *moral* advantages of such a system ought not to be overlooked. The industry it promotes, is favourable to the cultivation of every virtue; the constant interchange of benefits which it demands, cherishes and calls forth the benevolent affections; the immediate application of every attainment to a practical purpose, impressively teaches the important lesson, that intellectual superiority is valuable chiefly as a means of doing good to others; while the opportunity which extended responsibility affords, for the *manifestation* both of good and evil principles, is highly important as a means of discovering character, and of directing moral development.

52. In order to reap these advantages, however, the teacher must be himself an intelligent and good man; *thoroughly acquainted* with the system in all its bearings; and, perhaps I should add, *unfeignedly attached* to it as a mode of instruction. No man who is ignorant of the principles on which monitorial instruction rests, or who distrusts its capabilities, can possibly succeed in any extended application of it. Mr. Lancaster, in the exuberance of his zeal for this method, is reported to have said that, on his system an automaton might be a schoolmaster. If he did say so, it is only one of many remarkable proofs on record of the absurd lengths to which an extravagant admiration of that which is really good

in itself, will sometimes carry men. The truth is, as you well know, *a monitorial school requires a better and abler teacher than almost any other:* it demands more energy; more skill; more wisdom; and more strength both of body and mind: and hence it not unfrequently happens, that when schools fail to accomplish the expectations of their founders, reproaches are cast upon the plan, which really belong to the agent, who has been vainly attempting to carry out arrangements, to the management of which he was altogether incompetent.*

---

* All over Germany a prejudice is entertained, almost as universal as I hold it to be groundless, against any modification of the monitorial method of teaching. The nearest approach to it is, the employing of those who are pupils in the seminaries for teachers, to act the part of under masters in the primary schools, which are usually attached to those establishments; but there prevails, not among the people only, but among the educated and enlightened men of that country, a rooted aversion to the employment of one pupil to teach another. Hence the multiplication of masters is their idea of a perfect school. The larger the proportion of masters to the number of scholars, the better the system is conceived to be; and hence a rate of expenditure for the purposes of education, far beyond what can ever be looked for in Great Britain. Nor is the pecuniary objection the only one; for if this were a fit occasion, it would not be difficult to prove, that there is a quickening and improving energy in the monitorial method when it is skilfully applied, which no amount of masters nor increase of expenditure can adequately supply; that it brings into play principles,—left dormant under the teaching even of good masters,—which act most

53. In offering you a few hints on the selection, training, and government of monitors, I am anxious that you should feel that your success as a teacher, will almost entirely depend upon the amount of sagacity, skill, and wisdom, which you can bring to bear in this most delicate and difficult work. Mistakes here are fatal.

---

beneficially both on the monitor and his section of pupils, in promoting their progress and preparing them for the business of life; and that if this beneficial tendency has been but rarely exemplified, it is only another proof among many, how little advance can be made in the improvement of education, without the means of training masters to the knowledge and exercise of their profession.

In France the same prejudice against monitorial teaching does not prevail as in Germany, and great exertions have been made, with the countenance and aid of the government, to encourage and extend it. But, though there can be no doubt that the use of monitors has infused a spirit of alertness and activity into the French *écoles primaires,* which one feels the want of in the *volks-schulen* of Germany, yet the monitorial method is far from having attained in France its full development and efficiency. This is owing, in a great measure, to the notion which has gained ground even among schoolmasters over that country, that boys can be trusted with the teaching of nothing beyond the mechanical processes of reading, spelling, and ciphering. Of this opinion we have long had many practical refutations in schools established among ourselves, where much intellectual and even moral training is accomplished by means of monitors; and these schools, we may confidently anticipate, will serve as models in the preparation of any great legislative measure for the education of the English people. (*Pillans' Three Lectures,* 1836.)

54. Let me advise you then, prior to any open declaration of your choice, to obtain, by repeated individual examinations, and strict observation, an intimate acquaintance with the personal character and peculiarities, both mental and moral, of those boys on whom you have fixed your eye as appearing at first sight fit for monitorial employment. I need not say, that you will find it necessary always to have *in your mind*, and in your private memorandum book, a certain number of pupils, in this particular respect, *on trial*, out of which list you may from time to time fill up vacancies, as the parties are respectively tested, and found worthy of your confidence.

55. In deciding, however, upon this fitness, regard must be had to various qualifications. The quickest and best scholar is by no means certain to make the best monitor. You want other qualities besides talent. There must be patience, good temper, integrity, industry; and, along with steadiness of character, no small portion of *enthusiasm*, or little good will result from the appointment. Besides this, there should be some degree of *aptness to teach*, and a general willingness to follow out such directions as are laid down for the guidance and government of the school.

56. The same degree of care and discrimination must again be exercised, in reference to the particular *kind* of responsibility which is to be entrusted to particular individuals. A boy, who may

be quite unfit for the maintenance of order, or for carrying out general arrangements, will sometimes make an invaluable teacher of a single class; and, in like manner, while one is fitted by patience, and kindness, and ingenuity in illustration, for instructing the youngest and the most ignorant; another, by superior talent, weight of character, and ability to command, is better adapted for teaching and governing his equals in years and attainments. All these diversities of talent and character must be kept distinctly in mind,—*they must regulate your choice.*

57. In these appointments, you will find it advisable sometimes to consult the wishes of the boys themselves, as to the particular work which should be allotted to them. It is occasionally of great advantage to yield to these little preferences; it is *essential* to the success of any monitor that he should enter upon his work, not only with perfect good-will, but with alacrity and hope. Hence, the office should always be connected with reward; the service regarded as an honour, and employment esteemed a privilege. Where this is the case, an enthusiastic desire to bring forward the various classes committed to their charge, will not unfrequently be excited, inspired by which, difficulties of all kinds will be readily overcome, and an amount of knowledge be imparted, far beyond the most sanguine calculations of the teacher.

58. With all this care in selection, there must

also be connected appropriate training and government. *Authority* must be delegated little by little, and then only in connexion with diligent superintendence, and numerous checks against its abuse; and *instruction* must be imparted, not only to monitors in common with ordinary pupils, but apart,—alone,—at an hour when others are away, and with especial reference to their particular position and duties. In the acquisition of knowledge, *they*, above all others, must be directed to *principles;* for a monitor will teach well or ill, just in proportion to his acquaintance with, or ignorance of, the principles on which his instructions are based. And since it is by and through them chiefly that moral influences are to be imparted, it is of the utmost importance that they should be made sensible of the responsibilities which, by reason of their office, attach to their conduct and example. You will best accomplish this by taking them, to a certain extent, *into your confidence;* treating them always with respect; governing them with a mild but steady hand; and availing yourself of every opportunity for enlarging their minds, and impressing their hearts.

59. The following valuable remarks on the training of monitors, have been communicated to me by Mr. Crossley, the able superintendent of the Central school, whose long experience and distinguished success as a *monitorial* teacher entitle him to be heard with deference by those who are but just beginning the same course.

"A master's first thoughts on taking charge of a school, should be directed to the formation of a band of monitors. For this purpose, after selecting as nearly as he can, boys possessing suitable qualities, he will arrange his lessons according to the number of his drafts, which will, of course, depend on the number of his pupils. Having thus determined *on the number of his drafts,* and on the lessons to be studied at *each* draft, he will appoint a boy to the several stations to act as a monitor. The boy thus appointed, is supposed to be able to spell and to read the lessons, but possessing no knowledge of the business beyond these two qualifications; he is then first to be taught the meaning of each word, and to be exercised in giving illustrations of its varied application, both from Scripture, general history, science, and from subjects within the range of his pupils' observation. In some cases the pre-fixes, post-fixes, and roots of the words are important. He must then be exercised in *the art of questioning,* so as to be able to communicate his information by interrogation, and by that alone, and to keep up without any auxiliary stimulant the eager attention of his pupil. He must further be taught to vary his questions on the same word, so that repetition may not tire; and he must be instructed how to discover the proper instant to change from simultaneous repetition to individual examination, from brief description to rapid questioning, from the lively statement of facts, to the calm and impressive deduction of instructive lessons.

"In giving definitions, the *simplest* mode of expression must be carefully sought; which will, of course, generally be in Saxon phraseology. These definitions must be learned by the newly appointed monitors at the rate of about a dozen or twenty a day. The master must set apart a portion of each day, either from 12 to 1, (which usually is best,) or from 6 to 7 in the evening, to hear each individual repeat these meanings. In the first instance, it may be necessary to give up both these portions of time to the work. To accomplish his purpose, he must form his newly selected monitors into a draft; each, in turn, must then question on his own particular words, as he would do in the draft for which he is training. After the definition has been given, the questioner for the time being, must call for an instance of the application of the word, or an illustration containing some additional information more or less remotely connected with it. Here the master's reading, experience, and judgment, will find full scope; for when the boys fail, he should be ready to supply the desirable lesson, the parallel passage, the fact, or the opinion. In this way the monitor's mind is stored with numerous pertinent illustrations; he is exercised in applying them naturally and in familiar language; and instead of communicating in a formal manner and set style, he learns so to vary his observations as to avoid sameness. His mind thus disciplined will ever furnish him with new examples in his daily course of teaching. This plan must be followed daily till the whole of the lessons of each draft have been the subject of inquiry; nor must this practice be discontinued, until monitors can be chosen from among the boys who have themselves been taught by those who have thus been trained.

"I must, however, here enter a protest against the master's supposing that all is done when his monitors are trained; and, further, against his even supposing that they ever will be thoroughly trained by this or by any other method, except he can and does set them the example, both in the manner and in the spirit of teaching. He must, from the commencement, be daily seen teaching in the drafts, infusing into his monitors a spirit little short of enthusiasm, and showing himself a model both of what he wishes them to be and to do."

All this, it is evident, implies much labour and self-denial on the part of the master; it was not, therefore, without reason, that, in a former letter, I adopted Fellenberg's language, and claimed for this office, "*a vigilance that never sleeps, a perseverance that never tires.*"

60. But severer trials than any that have yet been mentioned, must occasionally be endured by the conscientious teacher of a monitorial school,—I mean those which are connected with the punishment, and, if necessary, the dismissal of his monitors. I have already referred to the opportunity which extended responsibility affords, for the *manifestation of evil* as well as of good principles, and I have ranked this means of discovering character among the advantages of the monitorial system. It is obvious, however, that it can only be so, in proportion as delinquency thus manifested, is followed by appropriate punishment. Monitors, by their office, are exposed to certain temptations from which others are exempt. Bribes of various kinds, in spite of every regulation to the contrary, will from time to time be offered and accepted; partiality will then be shown to one, and tyranny be exercised over another; falsehood will probably follow; and evils of the most tremendous character may, in this way, be fostered and indulged. It must be so while human nature continues as it is. But are we then to cast aside monitors altogether? By no means. It is better to *know* betimes that these dispositions exist, that we may apply remedies before it is too late. The great point is, to secure an *early* dis-

covery of unfaithfulness, and this is not so difficult as some are apt to imagine. A monitor's power is, after all, very limited; it is not like *fagging*, a secret and uncontrolled force, wielded by the stronger over the weaker; it is power *delegated* by the master, exercised only under his eye, and subjected to his superintendence; and moreover, held very frequently by the younger and the weaker, since neither physical strength nor mere intellectual vigour qualify for its reception. Originally trifling in amount, it is continually checked by perfect freedom of appeal to the teacher, who, it must be remembered, is all the while present in the room, and engaged chiefly in observing the conduct of these very agents. The consequence is, as experience has abundantly shown, bribery cannot long be concealed, falsehood is almost certain of immediate discovery, and the most petty acts of tyranny are reported almost as soon as committed. Still " offences will come," sometimes of the serious character to which I have already referred, and sometimes of a lighter description, such as ebullitions of temper, violence of language, disobedience to orders, neglect of duty, want of interest in the work, or the yielding of that which is merely " eye service." Now in such cases, especially those of the first-mentioned class, a teacher has no choice. Cost him what it may, he must dismiss the offender from his office. It may be the first transgression,—the delinquent may be the most intelligent and useful of monitors, he may be the very one on whom he has bestowed the greatest amount of labour, and therefore probably the boy he has loved best,—I repeat it, cost what it will, *he must cease to employ the unfaithful monitor, or his moral influence is fatally undermined.* Any punishment he may inflict on such a boy, will, from the circumstances of the case, be done with so much unfeigned sorrow, that there is the greatest reason to hope the offender will be more benefited by the deprivation than he could be by any other process. Lay it down, therefore, as an invariable rule, never to pass by the offences of a monitor; in no other way can you secure among them that habit of circumspection, and that high moral character, which is so essential to their usefulness.

61. I need scarcely add more. This brief letter is not intended to occupy the place of any existing manual for the regulation of monitorial schools, otherwise much would have to be added on other subjects, besides the selection and training of monitors. For the system to work well, there must be a careful and distinct classification of the school, for each separate department of study; and unceasing vigilance must be exercised to guard against some boys' being left in a position where they are dispirited by continual defeat; while others, who advance with ease, are injuriously detained in a class which demands from them no

energy or effort. But for these, and various other matters of detail, highly important as they are in themselves, and intimately connected, as they must be, with the general efficiency of a school, it is sufficient to refer you to the authorised publications of the two societies.

62. One objection, however, which is continually made against monitorial schools, deserves a passing notice. It is a matter of frequent complaint, that they are so often scenes of noise and of tumult. That this is a very serious evil cannot be denied; tranquillity and quietness would certainly be far preferable, if they could be attained without too great a sacrifice of time and improvement. But the truth is, noise is inseparable from the united employment of *numbers*, and there is no remedy for it but dispersion or listless indolence. A quick eye and ear will soon distinguish between the activity of business, and the irregular action of idle conversation; and a reasonable mind will see the folly of expecting that any community, labouring for a common object, should present the quietness of a convent, from which useful activity is banished.

63. To avoid needless prejudice, however, and to explain the true character of that apparent tumult which is occasioned by the hum of voices, and the excitement of mind, you should *invariably demand and obtain perfect silence, the instant that any*

stranger enters your school-room. By so doing, you can show him at once, that, whether in a state of activity or of rest, the order of the school is equally good, and your control the same. If you can *obtain* this required silence in an instant, without an effort, or an angry look; and if you can *retain* it as long as you please, without renewed and repeated commands, the most prejudiced man will see the reality of the distinction to which I have referred. Nay more, he will go away impressed by the exhibition of a power, which can, in one moment, bring order out of apparent confusion, and hold in check the activities of hundreds of minds, without drawing forth one tear, or even removing the smile of happiness from a single countenance. But if you cannot do this; if the command for silence must be repeated again and again; if frowns must be sent across the room, and looks of promised vengeance, before obedience can be obtained; if the moment after it is secured, restlessness meets the eye, and murmurings fill the ear, do not, I pray you, complain if your visitant, irritated by this evident want of control, should go away, and speak contemptuously both of you and your school. In vain will you protest that you *can* govern; in vain seek to attribute this "*unusual disorder*" to some momentary perversity on the part of the children; in vain will you appeal to their acquirements, or rest your defence upon a conscientious performance of duty; in the absence of *unlimited* control, all is vain and worthless. It matters little upon what system such a school may be conducted, it can never be efficient,—*the teacher is incompetent.*

LETTER V. TO THE SAME.

"DIDAKTIK," OR THE ART OF COMMUNICATING.

64. By this word *(didaktik)*, which the Germans have adopted from the Greek, I wish you to understand, *the art of teaching;* as distinguished on the one hand, from their *methodik*, or science of methods; and on the other from their *pädagogik*,* or science of education; of which, the art of communicating is only one part or division. You will readily perceive that it is an attainment perfectly distinct from any particular plan or system; and also a very different thing from what is usually termed, *tact in teaching.* It is in fact, the art of *so* communicating knowledge, that the pupil shall, as far as possible, comprehend in all its relations, the truth sought to be imparted; and that, associating what is thus received, with other and previous acquisitions, he may be led at one and the same

---

* Dr. Bryce (of Belfast) suggests the word padeutics, which may be considered both as an art and a science; an art when it lays down rules, a science when it teaches general principles.

time, "to cultivate his original faculties,"* and to store his mind richly and permanently with valuable facts. This is what I mean by "the art of teaching," a talent which few naturally possess, but which may doubtless be acquired by the careful and diligent study of the human mind, in connexion with a moderate share of "practice."

65. The use of this latter word suggests an analogy which, certainly to some extent, subsists between the profession of teaching and that of medicine. He who would be an accomplished physician, must study *principles*, as well as "see cases;" and, in like manner, he who would be a useful teacher, must look beyond systems to the principles on which they rest. The man who thinks himself qualified to teach, merely because he has observed others teaching on a particular plan, is just as much an empiric, as the medical pretender whose course of study has been limited to occasional walks through the wards of an hospital. It was in connexion with this view of the subject, (its relation to the philosophy of the human mind,) that Dr. Thomas Brown, of Edinburgh, spoke of the art of teaching as "the noblest, and in proportion to its value, the least studied of all the arts." When examined in this light, it cannot fail, I think, to be recognised as an attainment equally important to day and to Sunday school teachers; because, it

---

* "The business of education."—*Dugald Stewart.*

bears as directly on the effectual communication of Divine, as of secular knowledge.

66. After these remarks, from which you may gather the notions I entertain of the length and breadth of this subject, it is scarcely necessary for me to add, that a letter, like the present, can, of necessity, contain little more than a few brief hints, *relating* indeed to the art in question, but by no means sufficient for its entire comprehension. Before this can be accomplished, many a volume must be studied; and, let me say too, many a night passed in deep reflection upon the observations of the day.

67. I will suppose you then, actuated by a sincere desire to communicate instruction in the best possible way, entering your school-room, perplexed and harassed by the waywardness and indifference of your pupils; and that in this state of mind you put the question, "What can I do to excite attention, to stimulate dulness, to awaken effort?" I reply, in the first place, as preliminary indeed to every thing else,—bring distinctly before your own mind the well-known fact, that *children delight as much in exercising their minds as their limbs;* provided only that which is presented to them, be suited to their capacities, and adapted to their strength.*

---

* Probably it is no exaggeration to say that the appetite for knowledge is as great as any bodily appetite. To *know*, is one of the strongest desires of childhood; to obtain a new

68. "It was but this morning, (says a recent writer on education,) that I watched a young lazzaroni while he sought to make his little crazy boat lie straight and steady upon the water. How fertile was he in expedients; how ingenious in contrivances; how resolute against despair! First were the waves too strong; he sought out, therefore, a more sheltered spot: he next adjusted the balance and unfurled the sails—still without success. He then looked around him in much perplexity, till some of that long sea-weed, which is scattered over the coast after a storm, caught his eye: this he seized eagerly, and peeling it into long strips, he tied with them his little boat to a stone, (his sheet anchor;) and then wading as far out as the weed would permit, and so shaping his course that a neighbouring jetty might afford him smooth and tranquil water, he again placed his boat upon the sea. There he stood breathless, his hands busied with his burdens, his shirt tucked up and held by his teeth, but still half floating on the water, and his face troubled as though with his last hope. One moment he seemed to have succeeded; the next, and his boat again lay with its side upon the waves:

---

word is pleasant, and to gain a new idea is pleasanter still; but to be crammed with words without ideas is very painful. Dr. Johnson was anything but a philosopher, when he said that "no attention can be obtained from children without the infliction of pain." Happily for this generation, this notion is now nearly exploded.

he did not however even then despair, but sat himself upon the beach, with an old nail and a stone, to devise some other remedy."* Now, we have only to make *our* experiments equally *interesting* to the youthful mind, in order to excite and to sustain the same ardour.

69. It is a great mistake to suppose, as many do, that, in order to make learning pleasant to the young, difficulties must as much as possible be removed out of the way. On the contrary, it is in teaching them to *overcome* difficulties, that we shall be most likely to create the interest we are so desirous of calling forth. As a general rule, it should be the care of a teacher to supply his pupils from day to day with a succession of topics, somewhat *beyond their knowledge, without being above their comprehension.*

70. General rules, however, will not suffice for the guidance of young teachers; they want details, examples, illustrations; and without these, rules are worthless. If, therefore, I should sometimes enlarge on certain branches of instruction, with a minuteness which their relative importance would scarcely seem to justify; if I should stop to weigh conflicting opinions on points which may at first sight appear in themselves too trifling for discussion; if I should sometimes, for the sake of elucidation, descend to apparent littlenesses; remember

* Outline of a System of National Education. London, 1835.

that I do so, not because I am either regardless of the importance of condensation, or insensible to the offensiveness of puerility; but because I am determined in these letters to sacrifice every thing else to perspicuity and practical usefulness.

71. THE ALPHABET is usually the first subject presented to the notice of a child at school; and a more difficult or tiresome lesson he is never doomed to meet with in his whole future course. The *names* of the letters are unmeaning and arbitrary sounds; and with two or three exceptions, the *forms* are not associated with any object previously recognised. How can such an exercise be expected to produce anything but weariness and disgust? You will be glad to hear that men of the highest attainments in literature, have not thought it beneath their character and standing to endeavour at least to facilitate the passage across this " bridge of sighs."*

72. Mr. Wood, of the Sessional school, Edinburgh, whose views I shall first mention, attaches no importance to the *order* in which the letters are learned. He ridicules the idea of perplexing children at this period, with any division of the letters into vowels and consonants; or the still further

* " A palace and a prison on each hand."—(*Childe Harold.*) The communication between the ducal palace and the prisons of Venice is a gloomy bridge, or covered gallery, high above the water, and divided by a stone wall into a passage and a cell.

classification of consonants into *mutes, liquids, semivowels,* and *double consonants;* and he disapproves, as equally unsuited to their capacities, the distraction of their minds with *labials, dentals, gutturals,* and *nasals;* even though accompanied by the explanation, that these hard words mean nothing more than *lip, teeth, throat,* and *nose* sounds. No attempt, however, appears to have been made at the Sessional school, to remove the tedium invariably connected with this branch of instruction; unless, indeed, an artificial exhibition of the twenty-six letters on a box, contrived by the late Dr. Andrew Thompson, for the use of his own parish school, can be thus designated.

73. Professor Pillans, in some lectures which he delivered in the year 1827, on the theory and practice of teaching, proposes, on the contrary, to arrange the alphabetic characters in brotherhoods, according to the organs of voice used in pronouncing them; and to teach the child the knowledge of his letters at first, and for a long time, in this way only.

" We should thus avoid," he says, " the greatest difficulty the child encounters in learning the alphabet, that of recollecting the sequence or arrangement of the letters. Their order of succession in our common alphabet, is entirely capricious, and appears, indeed, to be purely accidental; and a knowledge of it, so far from being indispensable at the outset, is in that stage altogether useless for any practical purpose. Yet, in the ordinary way, the child is arrested, and unseasonably detained in the very porch of learning, by being compelled to name, and not to name only, but to learn by heart, a series of letters, which have not one associating tie to bind them in the memory, but juxta-position. It is stringing beads, as it were, on a thread of sand. It may be well he should know this alphabetic arrangement when he comes to consult a dictionary; but I really cannot see its use for any other purpose. On the other hand, by the classification of letters in their cognate relations, the acquisition of them may be made an amusing exercise. The attention of the child being drawn to the organs of voice employed in each set, he makes experiments upon them, in imitating the sounds he hears, and has thus a guide to the pronunciation of each letter, which greatly facilitates his acquaintance with their form and power." *

74. Jacotot, to whose principles and methods I shall hereafter have occasion to refer, meets the difficulty in by far the best manner; he gets rid of alphabetic teaching altogether, and introduces the pupil, from the first, to a knowledge of words. At the Borough Road school, the *principle* of dispensing with alphabetic teaching has long been adopted: the alphabet class has merged into that of children in *two letters;* and all unmeaning combinations have been utterly excluded. The advantage is obvious. If the word " me," " in," or " to," for instance, be mentioned, the child recognizes a familiar sound, and, judging by the ear, he almost intuitively answers, m-e, to the question, " Can you spell the word me?" If, after having mentioned the word, the monitor tells him to point

* Pillans' Letters to Kennedy.

on the lesson to the letters which compose it, his curiosity is excited, and the gratification attendant on a successful effort, excites a desire to encounter new difficulties.*

75. SPELLING. We learn to spell, chiefly, if not exclusively, in order that we may be able to write correctly; that method, therefore, which will most speedily and effectually enable us to carry the relative situations of the letters in the mind, so that whenever we wish to express our thoughts on paper, we can do so without misplacing them, is certainly the best. Now, as writing a word is a *slower* operation than *orally* spelling it; and as the mind is obliged in that exercise to dwell longer on the relative situation of every letter, than it is in mere

---

* The absurdity of teaching the letters of the alphabet by their arbitrary *names,* in place of their *sounds,* has long been felt in France and Germany. We tell a child to say, *pe-aytch-wi-es-i-see,* and then call upon him to pronounce it. What would he conclude, if he reasoned, but that it must be, *peaytchwiesisee,* and by what magic can he learn that it should be pronounced *fizik!* A striking illustration of this occurred in a school which I visited. Two bright children, of six years of age, could repeat *every letter* of a word at sight, and then would look up, with an innocent inquiring face to their teacher, unable to divine how this cabalistic combination of sounds should be pronounced together, until he repeated the word. It seems they had formerly been guided by the pictures of the objects annexed to the words, and had pronounced the name as they had learned to speak it. But, *the perfect knowledge of the letters* afforded no *clue* to the sound of the word.—*Woodbridge.*

pronunciation, the *orthography* of the word must be more deeply impressed on the memory by writing, than it can be in any other way. When, therefore, the learner has become able to write, this mode of teaching him to spell should by no means be neglected.

"Reading should invariably precede spelling. I do not mean that the child should be kept a long time in learning to read, before he commences spelling; but that he should never be set to spell a word until he has first become able readily to read it. The reason is, that reading is much easier than spelling, and that a person cannot spell, by thinking how a word *sounds,* but he must recollect how it *looks.* The eye, therefore, as well as the ear, must become familiar with a word before it can readily be spelled. One thing that renders reading easier than spelling is, that perception is more vivid and distinct than conception. Hence it is easier to distinguish two similar words, as *cat* and *rat,* or *eat* and *tea,* when the eye is fixed upon them in reading, than it is to recollect the difference in their orthography, when they are absent from the eye."*

76. These judicious remarks coincide in the main, with the substance of a lecture upon this branch of tuition, delivered by another practical teacher, before the convention of teachers, assembled to form the American Institute of Instruction in 1830. Both agree that the words to be spelled should first be embodied in reading lessons, and *afterwards* arranged in columns; and both insist that the *evidence* of their being possessed by the pupil should in all cases be rendered *in writing.* On this point the lecturer justly observes,—

* Parkhurst.

"In all branches susceptible of it, the exercises, the results of study, should be presented to the *eye*, as the best organ of communication with the mind. Whatever is acquired through this medium, is better retained than when entering through any other. It may be said, *the eye remembers*. It is more *attentive* than the ear. Its objects are not confused. It takes in a single and perfect image of what is placed before it, and transfers the picture to the mind. Hence all illustrations in our teaching which can possibly be addressed to this organ, should be so applied."*

77. It must, however, be remembered, that spelling has to be taught, not only in Sunday schools, where *writing* forms no part of the instruction communicated; but also to thousands in day schools, who do not remain long enough to write with that freedom which is necessary in order to put down sentences from dictation. These principles, therefore, however good under certain circumstances, will not admit of general application in schools for the poor. We cannot do without distinct lessons for oral spelling; so we must content ourselves with endeavouring to make the instruction imparted in this way as intellectual and as exciting as we can.

78. The plan pursued at the model-school in the Borough Road, which plan is fully explained in the Manual of the society, is perhaps the best that can be devised.

---

* Thayer. Since the above was written, this lecture and several others of a similar character, delivered in the United States, have been reprinted in this country, under the title of " the Schoolmaster," 2 vols. Knight, Ludgate Hill.

"The spelling lessons, which are printed in both roman and italic type, to exercise the children in reading various characters, exhibit a two-fold arrangement. The names of things are arranged under various heads, such as trades, measures, vegetables, quadrupeds, clothing, fruit, medicine, flowers, birds, &c.; and columns of other words are placed alphabetically. The last fifteen lessons of the set consist of a selection of words, approximating in sound, but differing in spelling and signification. They embrace the principal orthographical irregularities of the language. The whole set consists of sixty folio lessons, containing, besides four alphabets, nearly six thousand words; selected primarily for the purpose of communicating a complete knowledge of English orthography, and revised with the design of including a very extensive range of useful knowledge, and inducing habits of observation and inquiry. The plan of teaching is invariable throughout the series; the pupils are expected to spell, read, and explain every word. Suppose, for instance, the word to be "he." The first boy would say h, e—he; and the second boy would, without giving a regular definition, express his sense of its meaning. He may be supposed to say, "him;" or, "not me;" or, putting it in a sentence, say, "he is here." Any answer which indicates a knowledge of the word should be accepted, however homely either in language or illustration. The same remark applies to all the definitions they give: if the idea be correctly received, repeated demands for explanation will soon lead to more suitable language and more correct definitions. The two principal points to be attained by the pupil are, the comprehension of the meaning of the term, and the power of expressing that meaning in suitable language.

"The meanings of the words in the alphabetical columns, which are generally derivative, the pupils learn by being exercised in separating the prefixes and affixes, and then tracing the root through other combinations. For instance, the word "*retrospective;*" the monitor would say, "Separate it," and the boys would reply, *retro*, behind, *spect*, look, and *tion*, act or action. He would then say, "What is the meaning of the word *retrospection?*" and he would ask for other instances in which the root occurs. In-spect, pro-spect, spect-acle, circum-spect, re-spect, and other words would be given."*

79. The advantages of this system of interrogation are numerous and weighty. It teaches even the youngest child to *apply* every word as it is brought before him, from his earliest acquaintance with a written or printed language. It leads the mind direct from the words to the legitimate use of them, the communication of ideas. By inducing the child to draw on the resources of its own mind, it teaches him to compare, to discriminate, to judge; a process by which he is rendered capable of far greater mental exertion. It necessarily insures a habit of observation and scrutinizing inquiry; it occasions close application; and it constantly calls upon the master rather to restrain than to excite.

80. READING. It has often been observed, (and certainly not without sufficient reason,) that very few persons read well! To read simply and natu-

---

* See Manual of the System of Primary Instruction, pursued in the model-schools of the British and Foreign School Society. See also, on this subject, Wood's Account of the Edinburgh Sessional School. To Mr. Wood the cause of education is deeply indebted. He was certainly the first to call public attention to the importance of giving a more *intellectual* character to popular education; and by his unwearied exertions in the Sessional school he demonstrated the *practicability* of it.

rally,—with animation and expression, is indeed a high and rare attainment. What is generally called *good reading*, is in fact the very worst kind of reading; I mean that which calls the attention of the auditor from the subject of discourse, to the supposed taste and skill of the person who is pronouncing it. *Ars est celare artem.** The best window is that which least intercepts the prospect; and he is the best reader, who brings before us the mind of the author, unencumbered by the tints and tracery of his own style and manner. Still it must be remembered that, with most persons, reading is *an art*. I have sometimes heard very bad advice given on this subject, in terms like these,—" Do not trouble yourself about rules; read *naturally*, and you will read well." Now, the misfortune is, (and it is this which makes the advice bad,) very few do *naturally* read well. In artificial society scarcely any person is perfectly natural. *Nature* is simple, easy, dignified, and graceful in all her movements; but ploughmen and milk-maids, (children of nature, as sentimentalists call them,) are certainly not models of ease and grace. The air and bearing of a courtier, the *accomplished* pupil of the dancing master and the drill serjeant, is certainly far more unconstrained and free; it is more dignified and *natural*. In like manner, the best readers are those who have most diligently studied their art; studied it so well, that you do

---

* The perfection of art, is to conceal art.

not perceive they have ever studied it at all. You so thoroughly understand, and so sensibly feel the force of *what* they say, that you never think for a moment *how* they are saying it, and you never know the extent of your obligation to the care and labour of the elocutionist. In schools, little can be done beyond teaching the pupil to read in a plain and intelligent manner; to pronounce with general correctness; and to avoid offensive tones. You may probably wish to have a few rules, by attention to which, this degree of proficiency may, in most cases, be secured. I will only mention four.

81. (1.) *Take care that the pupil thoroughly understands that which he is directed to read.* This is absolutely essential to his success. If he do not fully comprehend the *thought,* how can he be expected adequately to express the language in which it may be clothed? Attention to this point is just as important in the lowest as in the highest class. Indeed it is *there* (in the lowest class) that the *habit* of fully comprehending in the mind that which is presented to the eye, must be formed. The great evil of putting before children unmeaning combinations of letters, such as "bla, ble, bli, blo, blu," and all the rest of this ridiculous tribe, is, that in reading them, a *habit* is formed of separating the sight and sound of words from sense, a habit which frequently cleaves to the mind long after the days of childhood have passed away. If, therefore, you would have a sentence well read, read so as to be

understood and felt by the hearer,—take care that the reader himself both understands and feels it. The *progress* of your pupils, too, will by this means be greatly facilitated. "He who is taught the habit of carrying the sense along with the sound, is armed with two forces instead of one, to grapple with the difficulties he encounters; the one, his knowledge of the letters and syllables, and the other, his knowledge of the story."*

82. (2.) *Remember that the tones and emphasis which we use in conversation, are those which form the basis of a good elocution.* Children should, therefore, be instructed to read *as they talk*. How often do you find young people describing, with an ease and vivacity which is truly charming, events which, if read by them in the very same terms from a book, would be insufferably dull and uninteresting!

83. (3.) *Guard your pupils against rapidity and loudness.* A rapid and noisy reader is, of all others, the most disagreeable; and, at the same time, the most unintelligible. Insist, therefore, upon a slow and distinct enunciation of every word; without securing which, it will be impossible to obtain correct pronunciation, good emphasis, or suitable intonation. Slow reading, in a subdued tone of voice, is always most agreeable and impressive; in the reading of Holy Scripture, the

* Pillans.

boisterous fluency which ignorant persons so frequently applaud, is irreverent and offensive.

84. (4.) *Do not permit too much to be read at one time.* A good teacher can profitably occupy twenty or thirty minutes over a page, without at all wearying his children. He will often have to say, " I perceive you do not quite understand that passage; read it again." Then he will require definitions of the leading words, their synonymes and their opposites; then perhaps he will have the sentence analysed or paraphrased; and after this, he will thoroughly explain every incidental allusion, whether geographical, historical, or biographical, which may be involved in the passage. All this, it may be, must be done before that which is read can be thoroughly understood; and he knows, (to return to the point whence we set out,) that until it *is* understood it can never be properly read.

85. INTERROGATION. Intimately connected with the point which I have been urging, is the practice of interrogation; the object of which, when rightly conducted, is twofold; first, to ascertain satisfactorily that *ideas*, in distinction from mere words, are received by the pupil; and, secondly, to afford opportunities for the communication of *incidental instruction*.

86. There is no way in which the correctness or incorrectness of a child's ideas on any subject can be so effectually ascertained, as by proposing a series of questions; their extent and bearing being

determined, for the most part, by the answers received. A teacher who has not been in the habit of doing this, can form no adequate notion of the amount of ignorance and misapprehension which this *ploughshare of the mind* will turn up. Miss Hamilton, I think, mentions the case of a gentleman, who, in his childhood, reading to his mother something about the *patriarchs*, stumbled at the hard word, and called it *partridges*. The good lady at once set him right as to the pronunciation, but never dreamt of telling him the meaning of the word; he therefore continued to associate the idea of a bird with it. Hence, the next time he encountered the word *patriarchal*, he again asked for assistance, exclaiming, " Here, mamma, here are these *queer fowls* again;" and to the latest day of his life, he declared, he could not get rid of the association.*

87. Now there are two methods in which this tendency to misconceive the meaning of words may

---

* Mr. Wood, in his account of the Sessional school, relates several ludicrous stories of a similar character; and in illustration of the absurd notions which prevail among the lowest orders of the people, as to the value of reading, apart from the power of comprehending the meaning of that which is read, quotes Tickell's lines on " the Hornbook."

> "The aged peasant on his latest bed
> Wished for a friend some godly book to read;
> The pious grandson thy known handle takes,
> And (eyes lift up) this savoury lecture makes;
> 'Great A,' he gravely reads; the important sound
> The empty walls and hollow roof rebound.
> The expiring ancient reared his drooping head,
> And thanked his stars that Hodge had learned to read."

be met; and both must, as far as possible, be brought to bear upon the evil. The *first* is,—VISIBLE ILLUSTRATIONS. Wherever the subject will admit of it, there is nothing equal to this kind of explanation. You will recollect an observation made some paragraphs back, " the eye remembers;" it might also be said, (although of course comparatively and subject to exception,) *the eye makes no mistakes*. A child has a very different, a much more perfect idea of that which it sees, than it can have of any thing which is incapable of being perceived by the senses; its *conceptions* are generally vague and indistinct.

88. Among the subjects which admit most easily of being explained by objects of sight, might be mentioned the various branches of natural history, and the physical sciences generally. In some of these the object itself can be called in, and in others detached portions of it. In the absence of the object itself, or any part of it, a model, a graphic representation, an outline, or a diagram, will suffice; but *something* of the kind must, if possible, be presented. Hence the importance of schools being provided with *specimens* of as many different things as possible, and of children being taught to cultivate habits of observation and inquiry. It is in many respects of the highest importance to teach children to discern the most minute differences and resemblances in objects which they can examine; the eye, the ear, the

touch, the taste, the smell, should all be educated, by exercise on a great variety of objects. If the perceptive faculties be not carefully cultivated, it is impossible that the conceptions of a child can be either ready or accurate.

89. An example of the striking effect of *specimens* in aiding the imagination, is thus related by an eye-witness. " When a delegation of one of the most savage of the western tribes, a few years since passed through Philadelphia, they were invited to visit the museum. Finding therein many of their quadruped acquaintance, with various implements of their own warfare, and a vast number of objects before unknown to them, they were naturally much delighted with the celebrated establishment, and expressed (as far as an Indian ever deigns to express it) their admiration of the novel spectacle. Divers ejaculations, and some obscure signs of relaxed gravity, were occasionally observable during their progress through the rooms, until they came to that part of the hall where the skeleton of the huge mastodon stood all at once revealed to their bewildered senses. The awe which seemed to come over them now deprived their tongues of utterance, and held their eyes fixed in the direction of the vast black bony structure, as if it had been an object of adoration. Such, it was said, their tribe are in the habit of regarding the mammoth; and, as it had all their lives before been merely a creature of the imagination,

or seen only in detached portions, its real bulk and proportions had probably never before been adequately conceived."

90. There will, however, sometimes be found matters of science, which we can neither bring before the eye, nor explain to the comprehension of a child, and these he must be taught to receive on the evidence of testimony. It is important to guard the youthful mind against that contracted habit of thinking and reasoning, which makes its own knowledge and extent of observation the standard of probability. It was under the influence of this narrow and sceptical spirit that Mr. Hume maintained, that a miracle being contrary to experience, could not be established by any human testimony. And it was with equal reason and propriety that the king of Siam, when informed by a foreigner at his court, that in some parts of Europe, at certain seasons of the year, water became so solid that an elephant might walk over it, told the narrator, without much ceremony, that he lied. In many cases, however, in the absence of ocular demonstration, it is possible to adopt an *analogous* fact or principle; and, wherever this can be done in the way of illustration, it is of course highly desirable. Had it happened that any one at the court of Siam had been acquainted with the properties of heat, and capable of performing the requisite experiments, the unbelief of his majesty might easily have been

removed, and his confidence in testimony fully restored.

91. But besides this mode of illustration, it is sometimes necessary to carry out to a considerable extent, the practice already referred to, (78) of accustoming the pupil to separate the prefixes and affixes of words, and to trace the root through other combinations. Let me, however, in connexion with this subject, earnestly warn you against pushing this kind of investigation too far. I have known some teachers, partly perhaps from vanity, and partly from ignorance, make themselves exceedingly ridiculous by attempting to meddle with Latin and Greek roots, before they were at all acquainted with either of these languages. To a certain, but *very limited* extent, this may be done with safety; beyond that limitation, the practice is manifestly absurd, and sure to lead all parties into error. The best advice that can be given to a young teacher on this subject probably is this,—" So long as you are unacquainted with Latin and Greek, confine your etymological researches to the simplest examples that are given in elementary books prepared for this purpose; when you have mastered these languages, you may go as far as you please."

92. INCIDENTAL TEACHING, by which I mean the practice of communicating general knowledge in an incidental and unsystematic manner, although not liable to the same abuse, still needs to be imparted with judgment and caution. It should never be

forgotten, that in science, as well as in religion, there are many things which a "babe" in knowledge is "not able to bear." Some teachers, in the plenitude of their zeal to impart, or rather perhaps in their anxiety to *display*, are accustomed to cram mere children with a kind of food, which their tender minds can never digest. This is on every account highly objectionable. "It *brushes off* (as professor Pillans beautifully says) *the bloom* of interest and novelty from those sublime discoveries, which should be left to reward the learner, at a more advanced period of laborious and successful study. When there is in the world around us so much to be known that comes home to the business and bosom of the child, it is a great mistake to involve him in the intricacies of the solar system, to talk to him of orbit and gravity, parallax and disturbing forces, or even of ecliptic, equator, and meridian, at an age when his mind cannot possibly go beyond the figure on the map or board; and when the planetarium itself, if there happen to be one, is to him nothing more than a plaything. To set children a chattering about oxygen, hydrogen, caloric, and all the mysteries (as they must be to them) of modern chemistry, is education run mad; and, in truth, not less to be deprecated than the opposite extreme of the no-meaning system."* And even if understood, such knowledge is little worth.

* Letters to Kennedy.

The mere accumulation of facts in the memory is of trifling value, if unaccompanied by the development and training of the faculties. A mind filled with the results of other men's research, and unacquainted with the steps and processes of the proof, may, as Beattie remarks, fitly enough be compared to a well-filled granary, but bears no resemblance to the fruitful field, which multiplies that which is cast into its lap a thousand fold.

93. Having thus, briefly laid down the general plan on which you should proceed, in your endeavours to make that which is read fully understood, both by interrogation and illustration, I cannot do better than recommend you to study, as an exemplification of the *principles* I have endeavoured to enforce, a specimen of this kind of teaching, as it is actually carried out in the Borough Road school. You will find it in the Appendix.* It is an extract from the Educational Magazine, and was drawn up for that work by the editor, under the title of "A Day at the Borough Road School." This specimen, relating, as it chiefly does, to the impartation of scriptural instruction, will not be unacceptable to Sunday school teachers. They will see how diversified instruction may be, without at all losing its *religious* character; and they will feel, I trust, more than ever, that, *in order to do children good*, it is necessary to interest them. Tediousness in the

---

* Appendix B.

communication of religious instruction, (and every thing is tedious which is not understood) is absolutely mischievous; it occasions disgust, where we want to produce attachment; and, in the clumsy attempt to *force* an entrance for truth, it closes up the only avenue to the conscience and the heart.

94. WRITING.—On this subject a very few hints must suffice. First, then, with regard to *classification*, remember, that as writing is merely imitative, the best way to promote general improvement is, *to place beginners indiscriminately among good writers.* You will lose nothing by this arrangement, if you aim, as you should do, rather at making good writing *general* in your school, than at producing excellence in a few of the senior pupils. (2.) Bear in mind, that your pupil's success mainly depends upon the attention paid to him when *first beginning* to write. It is then that habits are formed, which he will find it afterwards almost impossible to alter. (3.) Let writing on slate, precede the use of pen and paper. The forms and combinations of letters will most readily be attained in this way; and when that is done, no great difficulty will be found in accustoming the pupil to the use of the pen. (4.) Let not the pupil attempt what is termed "small hand," until he can write a good bold text hand with neatness and accuracy. (5.) When he comes to learn the current or running hand, let him be taught that neither legibility nor

elegance will do without *expedition*. Accustom him, therefore, to write freely from dictation.

95. The most approved rules for preserving a right position of the body, for holding the pen, and for effecting the various movements and combinations by which the letters are to be executed, though highly important for you to know, would yet be out of place here. For these particulars you must study the best treatises on the art of penmanship.

96. The only other points to which it is necessary for me to allude, are these. (1.) Materials for writing should be of good quality,—it is not economical to use inferior articles. Steel pens, which may now be purchased at a very reasonable rate, are in every respect preferable to those which are made from quills; they are cheaper, they need no mending, and they execute the letters with greater neatness and precision. (2.) Every *line* should be examined as it is written. The habit which prevails in some schools, of writing a *page* before examination, is highly pernicious; quality in writing should at all times be regarded rather than quantity.

97. ARITHMETIC.—In teaching arithmetic, regard must be had to the same *great principles* which have already been laid down in relation to other branches of knowledge. Nothing must be considered as done, that is not thoroughly comprehended; a *meaning* and a *reason*, must be attached to every step of the process. Begin, therefore, first of all,

by referring the pupil to *sensible objects,* and teach him to compute what he can see, before you perplex him with abstract conceptions. A mere infant may in this way be taught to add, subtract, multiply, and divide, to a considerable extent. Apparatus for this purpose, of various kinds, is already in use; but what need have you of apparatus? Every thing around you and about you may be made subservient to this end.

98. It will not do, however, to stop here. The mind *must* before long be accustomed to abstractions, and therefore the sooner you can teach a child to convert this tangible arithmetic into abstractions the better. You will do this to some extent, by drawing its attention to what has been called, aptly enough, " *the process of disentanglement.*"

"You take a skein of ruffled thread; and, if you can find the end, you carefully draw it through all its loops and knots, and in a few minutes it is unravelled. Now just in this manner must the minds of children be exercised in finding out the truth of some abstract proposition. To a mind not so exercised, a very simple question will be extremely formidable. How often have not only children, but their elders, been puzzled by the simple question, 'What is two-thirds of three-fourths of any thing?' Now to get at the truth required here, it will be seen how necessary it is to get at that part of the proposition that can be laid hold of; that is to say, the part which the mind can *attach,* from its being something known: it would in this case, of course, see first that the three-fourths were *three quarters;* and then it would soon discover that *two quarters,* the two-thirds of them, must be half. We give

"DIDAKTIK," OR THE ART OF COMMUNICATING. 89

this and other illustrations, to show that, by applying the analytic process properly, a very small quantity of real knowledge will produce a very large proportion of arithmetical power; therefore it is not so much the knowledge that may be fixed dogmatically in the mind, that will serve your purpose, as that which the mind itself evolves in its process of elaboration. It will be the business of the teacher to help the mind to create its own strength, and this he will do by subjecting it to wholesome and judicious exercise."*

99. *Take care that your pupil never proceeds to a second example in any rule, until you are quite sure that he thoroughly understands the first.* No matter what time may be consumed upon this introductory effort,—he must not be allowed to go on with partial and inaccurate notions of what he is about. You will often be deceived in this particular. It is necessary, therefore, when a result is obtained, to require an explanation of every step by which it has been reached; to demand *why* that particular course, in preference to any other, should have been pursued; and to ascertain whether the pupil so far understands the *reasons* of the process, that he could, if he chose, in conformity with those reasons, adopt other modes for arriving at the same conclusion.

"Two persons never have exactly the same associations of ideas; they never associate their ideas in exactly the same order. The consequence is, that no two persons think of the same proposition alike. Hence, a proposition expressed in

---

* Educational Magazine.—Method of Teaching Mental Arithmetic.

certain terms, may be very clear and intelligible to one person, and very obscure, or altogether unintelligible, to another; and perhaps, with a very slight change of terms, the case would be entirely changed. It would be intelligible to the latter, and unintelligible to the former. An explanation which is very clear and lucid to one, will often convey no idea at all to another. When a proposition is made for two persons to reason upon, they will often take it up and manage it very differently in their minds. When the subject is such as to admit of demonstration, as is the case with mathematics, they will generally come to the same conclusions. But on other subjects their conclusions will sometimes agree and sometimes not. There are several valuable practical results to be derived from this. First, it is very important that a teacher should be able readily to trace, not only his own associations, but those of all his pupils. When a proposition or question is made to a scholar, he ought to be able to discover at once whether the scholar understands it or not. If he does not understand it, the teacher should be able to discover the reason why, and then he can apply the remedy. This is to be done only by questioning the scholar and tracing his associations, and finding out what he is thinking about, and how he is thinking about it. Without doing this, the teacher is as likely to perplex the scholar as to assist him by his explanations. Secondly, when the scholar does not understand the question or proposition, he should be allowed to reason upon it in his own way, and agreeably to his own associations. Whether his way is the best or not on the whole, it is the best way for him at first, and he ought by no means to be interrupted in it, or forced out of it. If teachers would have patience to listen to their scholars, and examine their operations, they would frequently discover very good ways that had never occurred to them before."*

---

* Colburn's Lecture on Teaching Arithmetic.

"DIDAKTIK," OR THE ART OF COMMUNICATING.

100. It is to the variety of methods used in obtaining the results, coupled with the pupil's subsequent reasoning on the correctness of the principles which he has selected, that it is usual to look at the Central school in the Borough Road, for proof of the reality of those attainments which astonish every visitor. Rules which are seldom *understood,* and scarcely ever viewed in connexion with the principles on which they are based, are of little use to children. The business of the teacher is, *not* to send his pupil to an unintelligible rule, but first to make him see the *difficulties* of the question which has baffled his ingenuity; then to lead him on, *by a succession of questions,* to discern the *principle* he is in search of; and, finally, to let truth so break upon his mind, that, by the possession of it, he may be only incited to pursue with fresh vigour other and more difficult investigations. Arithmetic thus taught, becomes a fine mental discipline, and strengthens the intellectual powers, instead of resting only in the memory.*

101. But in order to carry on this mode of tuition, *your own explanations must be clear and simple.* "Will you please to tell me why I carry one for every ten?" said a child to her instructor. "Yes," replied he, kindly, "it is because numbers increase from right to left in a decimal ratio." The child sat,

---

* See Manual of the British and Foreign School Society.

repeated the information she had received to herself two or three times, and then looked sad. The master, as soon as he had answered, pursued his other business, and did not notice her. She was disappointed. She understood him no better than if he had used words in another language. "Decimal," and "Ratio," were words that might have fallen on her ear before; but if so, she understood them none the better for it. She looked in the dictionary, and was disappointed again; and, after some time, put away her arithmetic. When asked why she did so, she replied, "I don't like to study it, I cannot understand it."* I may safely leave you to make the application.

102. Again. *You should never underrate the difficulties of your pupils.* A child will not apply vigorously, unless it sees that its efforts are appreciated; unless it perceives that you recognise the difference between its capacity and your own. The *attention* which such an one can give to a difficult process is at best but limited; the intellect is soon exhausted, and the effort it makes is often painful while it lasts. Do not then strain the muscles of its mind, or cause its little feet to bleed, by an unreasonable forgetfulness, either of its short footsteps, or of the difficulties of the way. "A good schoolmaster," says old Fuller, "minces his pre-

* Hall's Lectures to Schoolmasters on Teaching.

"DIDAKTIK," OR THE ART OF COMMUNICATING. 93

cepts for children to swallow, hanging clogs on the nimbleness of his own soul, that his scholars may go along with him."

103. In the working of arithmetical questions, two points must be kept constantly in view,—correctness and dispatch. The attainment of the latter is often a matter of great difficulty. To supply this defect, (the want of rapidity,) contracted methods on slate should be encouraged, such as bringing any number of tons, hundred weights, quarters, and pounds, into pounds, in one line; working by aliquot parts and approximations; or calculating part of a question abstractedly, and part on the slate. A great variety of questions should also be given specially for pure mental solution.

"In performing these mental operations, although elliptical modes may be sometimes suggested, yet it is better to leave each pupil at liberty to calculate according to his own particular method. If, for instance, the question proposed to a class be, 'What shall I spend in a year of 365 days, at an average of 5d. a-day?' Some boys would solve it by noting 365 pence as £1. 10s. 5d. and by multiplying by 5, beginning at the pounds: others, prompt at multiplying and ready at the pence table, would almost intuitively see that $365 \times 5 = 1825 = $ £7. 12s. 1d.; while another might choose to obtain the same result by adding 365 fourpences and 365 pence, or 365 sixpences—365 pence.

"The talent of the *mental* arithmetician for practical purposes, is shown rather in detecting and promptly seizing on any aliquot parts, or favourable combinations of numbers, than in a capability of pursuing a lengthened course of involutions, or by the power of retaining and modifying long series of figures. Suppose the question to be, 'What is the interest of £576. 18s. 9d. for 8⅓ years, at 4 per cent. per annum? The boy who should detect that 4 times 8⅓ equalled 33⅓, which is the third of a hundred, and thus obtain his result by instantly dividing £576. 18s. 9d. by 3, would be much superior to him who found it necessary to go through the prescribed formula, although he might be well able to accomplish the extra labour."*

104. I need only further suggest on this subject, the importance of guarding the pupil against lassitude and inattention. To this end, *take care that your questions follow one another with the utmost rapidity.* If long pauses are permitted between questions, the children are sure to fill up the interval with thoughts not at all in accordance with the subject before them. You must allow them no *time* to wander. It is obvious, however, that such an exercise cannot be long continued. Fifteen or twenty minutes is quite sufficient at once; the moment the mind flags, it is time to stop. You will gain nothing by straining faculties, which can never be exercised beneficially but in a healthy state. This remark, I need scarcely say, applies to every other branch of learning, just as much as to

---

* See Manual of the British and Foreign School Society. I have preferred taking the *examples* given in this volume, as well as the principles, because new examples would throw no additional light on them, and because it should be *known* that this revised edition of the Manual is something far better than a mere directory for mechanical movements.

arithmetic. We can scarcely commit a greater error in education, than that of wearying the attention by attempting too much at once. Progress in any intellectual pursuit depends, much more upon intensity of application, than upon protracted study. To produce languor by over-working the mind, is to inflict a very deep and serious injury; such a resnlt should therefore most anxiously be avoided.

105. GRAMMAR. " I learned grammar (says William Cobbett) when I was a private soldier on the pay of sixpence a-day. The edge of my berth, or that of my guard bed, was my seat to study in; my knapsack was my bookcase, and a bit of board lying on my lap was my writing-table. I had no money to purchase candle or oil; in winter time it was rarely that I could get any evening light but that of *the fire*, and only my *turn* even of that. To buy a pen or a sheet of paper, I was compelled to forego some portion of *food*, though in a state of half starvation; I had no moment of time that I could call my own; and I had to read and write amidst the talking, laughing, singing, whistling and bawling, of at least half a score of the most thoughtless of men, and that too in the hours of their freedom from all control. And, I say, if I, under circumstances like these, could encounter and overcome the task, is there, can there be, in the whole world, a youth to find an excuse for the non-performance?"

106. But before either a youth or a child will heartily set about this task, he must be convinced of its utility; and he must be made to understand the nature and object of the study. On this point a great deal of misapprehension prevails. A boy who is presented with a string of definitions and rules, without being made acquainted with the principles on which these rules depend, never dreams that the dull lesson naturally arises out of the constitution of the very language he is using every day. It never once occurs to him, that the English *tongue* controls the English *grammar;* he imagines, on the contrary, that grammar gives the law, and that language must obey.

107. Perhaps he might be set right on this matter most readily, by its being briefly explained to him, how a missionary, for instance, thrown among a barbarous people, having an *unwritten* language, would proceed in order to form a grammar of that language. He might easily be made to understand how the whole procedure of the missionary would be guided and controlled by the usage of the barbarians; that he must take his laws from their practice; that he could not, in any case, *give* laws to them. In short, that his sole province as a grammarian would be, to ascertain and unfold, to classify and embody, existing usages.

108. It is precisely on this principle that Gram-

mar is taught at the Borough Road. The information (which is conveyed orally) is imparted in connexion with questions grounded on this view of the subject.

"The monitor would probably commence the conversation by remarking, in as clear a manner as possible, that every word in the language, like every boy in the school, belongs to some class. Stopping some seconds to ascertain that this simple fact was well understood, he might remark, that the only difference is, that there are eight classes of boys in the school, but nine classes of words. This would be followed by saying, 'Tell me the names of any things you see.' A number of things being named, he would say, 'Tell me the names of some things which you cannot see.' Several being mentioned, the question would be put, 'What have you told me about these things?' *Ans.* 'Their names.' Now the monitor would observe, all these names which you have mentioned belong to one class; the name of that class is, '*Nouns*;' all names belong to it, for the word Noun means Name. 'Goodness,' 'Justice,' 'Height,' 'Depth,' 'Length and Breadth,' and every name you can possibly find, even 'Nothing' itself belongs therefore to this class, because it and all these are names.

"Having proceeded thus far, he would judge it desirable to retrace his steps, to ascertain if he were thoroughly understood. He would therefore ask one, a dull boy in the draft, 'How many classes of words are there?' Another, 'What is the name of the class of words about which we have been speaking?' A third, 'What is the meaning of the word Noun?' A fourth would be asked to mention some name which did not belong to it; a fifth, what part of speech Nothing was. In this manner the monitor would ascertain if the attention of the class had been effectually directed to him. Pursuing his subject, he would ask them to mention a name. Supposing 'desk,' to be mentioned, the question would follow, 'Tell me something about desk.' They would mention long, narrow, wooden, strong, and other qualities, in rapid succession. The draft thus exercised would be led to discover that these are qualities, and although intimately connected with, are not nouns themselves. To assign these to another class, and to give it the name of '*Adjective*,' proposing some questions to insure his being thoroughly understood, would be his next object.

"The verb would be introduced, by asking them to tell him some word which implied motion. 'Fly,' 'run,' 'go,' and many others being given, he would class them under the name of '*Verbs*.' Some general questions would again ensue.

"Proceeding with his subject, he would ask them to mention one of the verbs they had just named; perhaps 'speak' would be selected. 'Tell me,' he would say, 'how I speak?' *Ans.* 'Slowly.'—*Quest.* 'In what other ways might a person speak?' *Ans.* 'Quickly, loudly, softly, intelligibly, roughly.'—*Quest.* 'What do all these express?' *Ans.* 'The manner of speaking.' Remember, then, all words which express the manner of acting are ranked in a separate class called '*Adverbs*.'—*Quest.* 'What is the meaning of the word Ad-verb?' *Ans.* 'To a verb.'—*Quest.* 'What is the difference between an adjective and an adverb?' *Ans.* 'An adjective expresses the quality of a noun, an adverb the quality of a verb.'—*Quest.* 'Is it correct to say the sea is smoothly?' *Ans.* 'No.'—*Quest.* 'Why?' *Ans.* 'Because sea is a noun, and requires an adjective.'—*Quest.* 'If I speak of the sailing of a ship, must I use the word calm or calmly?' *Ans.* 'Calmly.' —*Quest.* 'Why?' *Ans.* 'Because sailing is an action.'

"The *Pronoun* is of very easy introduction; its name 'for a noun,' sufficiently expresses its use, and a few examples are all that in this stage of the business is necessary. The *Articles* require only naming, referring to a few instances in which they are used; and *Interjections* are as readily distinguished.

"The distinctions of these seven parts being well impressed on the mind of the pupils, the monitor proceeds to the remaining two, which at the first glance, do not appear to admit of a very clear separation. The one is illustrated by the monitor's taking a slate in his hand, and saying, 'Tell me all the words you can think of, which express situation in reference to this slate.' The answers, 'above,' 'below,' 'under,' &c., will bring forth the *Prepositions*, and a reference to a hinge, will explain the *Conjunction*, which, when the other eight are known, requires no further distinction.

"When the class has arrived at this point, the monitor reads some sentences from his book, and requires each boy in turn to class the words, and give his reasons. Being well prepared for this exercise, it is rarely of long continuance. In the ensuing lessons it would be observed that the articles, —the gender, and properties of nouns,—the degrees of comparison in adjectives and adverbs,—the kind of verbs, and the varieties of the pronoun, have all relation to the number three. This presents an opportunity of giving a sure and ready index to these variations, which so often and so long perplex master and pupils. Thus learned, they are obtained at once and for ever.

" The influence of one word on another, or syntactical parsing, is now easily unfolded. A sentence being read, the monitor, at his discretion, makes various alterations in its construction, each of which is made the subject of inquiry. Care being taken that the difficulties are seen and felt, the monitor gradually leads the pupils by questions to their elucidation. Other sentences of a similar kind are then introduced, and the rule comes in as the result of their own observation and inquiry. It is thus seen to rise necessarily out of the language, instead of being arbitrary and indefinite; and so far from being a burden on the memory, and exciting disgust, it is welcomed as the result of a clear investigation, and cherished in the memory, from a thorough conviction of its truth and suitability."

A specimen of the *mode* of examination in this branch will be found in the Appendix.*

109. GEOGRAPHY. All practical writers, of any value, now agree that the best mode of imparting instruction in geography is, *to begin at home;* to teach a child the geography of its own parish, county, and country, before you attempt to introduce it to other parts of the world. It is obvious, that a learner can form no clear conception of the height of mountains, of the course of rivers, or of the nature of the great divisions of the earth, excepting as he can compare what he reads with that which he sees around him. Nothing, therefore, can be more absurd than to *begin* by introducing a child to the map of the world; or to go on filling its head with geographical descriptions of Africa, China, or Russian Tartary, before it is at all acquainted with England and her dependencies. In like manner, if you wish a child to have correct notions about lakes, islands, or isthmuses, you will be much more likely to insure his possessing them, by referring him to the peculiarities of a neighbouring pond or rivulet, than by any abstract description whatsoever. The *name* of mountain, and valley, and lake, and river, should indeed be invariably connected with the observation of hill and hollow, pond and brook.

110. Again, with regard to the relative situation

---

* Appendix B.

of distant places, a knowledge of which can only be obtained through maps, remember, that the pupil will only gain *knowledge* from looking at a map, in proportion as he is taught to associate the lines and spots of the map with the objects they represent. It is of no use setting him to gaze at dots, to remember their situations on the paper, or to recite the name attached to them in the book; unless the mind be accustomed at the same time to realise the objects they denote, and to recognise all this arrangement on paper, as nothing more than an aid to the imagination.

" We have had," says an able writer, " the details of an instance in which a child of two years old, could point to every line and spot upon the map of Europe, only on hearing its name, before he could yet pronounce a word. But while we mourn over the mistaken kindness which could thus prepare an infant for the premature grave to which he descended, we do not envy the reputation of that teacher, who would be satisfied with making his pupils equally expert in this parrot-like exercise. We fear there are many such instances; nay, we suspect there are many schools where the ideas derived from the map, are just such as would be obtained from studying those charts of human life which represent an event by a promontory, difficulty by a whirlpool, and death by a torrent or waterfall, terminating in the beautifully ornamented border, that surrounds this picture of time and history! We are only less liable to be imposed upon by that which pretends to represent invisible things.

" The first step necessary to enable the pupil to acquire ideas from representation, is to teach him the relation of the one to the other. Even the effect of pictures is often lost upon the young mind for want of a practical knowledge, or perception of perspective; and he supposes objects smaller or higher, from their appearance on the picture, or darker from their shade, because he has never been taught to observe the effect of distance and light. How much more liable is he to error, in regard to the naked outlines, or mere indices of great objects, presented on a map! I know not any mode so effectual to make the pupil familiar with the nature of maps, as to teach him to construct them from nature, and this may be accomplished, at the same time that he is learning to observe the objects around him.

" Let the course of observation to which we have referred, be extended to every thing within his horizon, and let him learn the individual name attached to every object of importance. Let him learn to observe them from different points of view. Point out to him the varying position of the sun. Let him observe its direction in the morning, at noon, and at evening,—and then show him the north star, and he will thus find the marks for the four standard points to which he is to refer all descriptions of the situations of places. Let the terms *east*, *south*, *west*, and *north*, be attached to these points, *only when he has learned the need of them;* and not be employed before he has acquired distinct ideas of them. Let him observe the direction of the great objects of the landscape, first from one prominent point, then from another. Let him notice those which are in a range or '*row*' with each other from his station—those which are on opposite sides—those which would form a triangle—and those which would make a square, or a cross, and thus fix the positions of every important place in his mind, so that he could sketch a map of these points and lines from his imagination as well as from direct perception.

" But he must in the mean time be taught the construction of maps of a much smaller space. Let him draw upon the slate, no matter how rudely, a square to represent the table upon which he is writing, or the room in which he is sitting. If practicable, let him look down upon it from the ceiling above; but in any event, let him mark the spot on which every object is placed, with its size and shape, as it *would appear* from above. As soon as he has repeated this so often, that he perceives the want of accuracy in his rude representations, furnish him with a scale to measure the room or the table, and the distance of the respective objects from each other; and supply him with a smaller rule, adapted to the size of his slate, divided into an equal number of parts. Then direct him to transfer, after the measurement of every line or distance with the larger rule, an equal number of parts with the smaller upon his slate, until every object is represented in proportionate size, and relative situation, with a good degree of accuracy. This he will be told is a *plan*, or *map*; and as his observations abroad are going on, he will probably be himself anxious to employ the same method to represent the various objects of the landscape before him. He should be led on, however, by graduated steps. Let him draw an entire plan of the house in which he lives, of the garden attached to it, and of the farm, or grounds around it. So far as it is practicable, let every effort be followed by *measurement*, as in the map of a room, in order that the habit of accurate observation, so valuable in life, may be cultivated, at the same time that he acquires the correct idea of distances.

" The pupil will now be prepared to delineate with more or less accuracy, the outlines of the country around him, and by observing carefully the ranges of objects, he may arrive at a tolerable degree of accuracy by mere inspection. He should be accustomed also to ascertain short distances by paces, and longer ones by an accurate observation of the time which is spent in passing over them, either on foot or in a carriage, and to register all the circumstances which are necessary for his map. As his perception of accuracy increases, he may be taught to trace the deviations from a straight line in a stream or a road; and if circumstances admit, he should be allowed the use of a chain or tape measure and a compass, as soon as he is capable of employing them.

"Such is the course it is desirable to pursue, in order to be fully prepared for the study of maps; and I know not how we can otherwise avoid the danger of false or imperfect conceptions, which will destroy half their value to the pupil. It is obvious, that it might be, and ought to be, commenced in the nursery, under the direction of the mother. It would serve as the amusement of many a listless moment, as soon as the child can use a slate and pencil. It might be carried on by any parent, who can spend two or three hours in a week with his children, before they are ten years of age. If they are left to begin at school, no reason can be given why it should not be adopted by the instructor of a boarding-school. Indeed, there are few teachers of common schools, whose influence and usefulness with their pupils would not be increased, and whose labour would not be on the whole lightened, by the extra lessons and little excursions which it would render necessary.

"After the pupil has become familiar with the construction of these simple maps, he should be taught to draw them on every variety of scale, until he ceases to think of the size of the map before him, and by immediate reference to the scale of measurement, should learn to perceive at once, through the medium of a map, the great objects which it represents, instead of the lines and points upon its surface, just as we perceive ideas through the medium of words. It will also facilitate his transition to other maps, if he be accustomed to draw a meridian through some prominent object, from an observation of the north-star, or a shadow at noonday; and to divide the map by other lines, drawn parallel and perpendicular to it, at regular distances. It will aid still farther in his transitions, if the central line from east to west be assumed as an *equator*, and distances be reckoned in both directions, from this and the first meridian.

"It is scarcely necessary to add, that as no description can be equally useful with the view of objects themselves, it is desirable that the pupil should learn the geography of the neighbouring country, as well as his own town, as much as possible, from *personal observation*, and be accustomed to describe and delineate its outlines. It should only be after his own sketches are executed, that he should be furnished with more complete engraved maps of the same region.

" Let me not be told that this is *theory*, plausible upon paper, but impracticable in its execution. It is but the *history* of what *has been done* and *still is done*, in the schools of Pestalozzi and his followers in Europe; and is in substance what must be done, by every one who is designed to be a topographical or military engineer. It would require little more time, thus to learn to delineate the great features of a country, if it were commenced at an early period, than it now does to imitate the letters of the alphabet. Every step is, in itself, perfectly practicable and easy. Only time and patience are necessary to combine them all, in an ordinary course of instruction. Where either of these fail, or where prejudice and avarice prevent the overtasked instructor from adopting this entire course, much may be done by devoting two or three hours in a week, for a short period, to this object. Some measures of this kind should always be taken, to prevent the blunders to which the uninitiated pupil is continually liable." *

111. GEOMETRY, the elements of NATURAL PHILOSOPHY, LINEAR DRAWING, and several other branches of knowledge, which are now introduced with great advantage into schools, fall under the same

---

* I am sure no apology will be necessary for this long extract from a lecture delivered before the American Institute of Instruction, by the Rev. W. C. Woodbridge. I am unwilling to keep back a paper so likely to be valuable, in order to make room for any observations of my own. I perfectly agree with him in what he has advanced; the principle is fully adopted in the Borough School.

general principles. The limits which I have thought it most expedient to prescribe for myself, will not allow of any lengthened observations on the best modes of teaching them. In all it will be found desirable, first to awaken, and then to gratify curiosity. Visible illustrations should, if possible, be presented. A cone cut into its several sections, viz. the circle, ellipse, triangle, parabola, and hyperbola, will render important aid in getting clear and distinct impressions of the elementary principles of conic sections; and a cube, and the various species of parallelopipeds, may be laid before a child with great advantage, in imparting the first principles of solid measure. " How few (says the writer I have so frequently quoted) in our schools, or among farmers or mechanics, have a clear and distinct idea of what is meant by a cube, or solid inch, or foot, or mile! And, until a person has a clear conception of that original elementary idea in solids, how can he move one step on the subject, except by groping in midnight darkness? And how is he to gain a conception of that idea, except by some familiar practical illustration? Three or four years ago, a gentleman sold a right of some water for carrying a mill. The quantity first agreed upon, was a stream which could be discharged through a two-inch tube. When asked what he should charge for the quantity which could pass through a four-inch tube, he answered, ' Twice the price of the other.' The purchaser, of course, obtained four times the water for twice the money, as a tax upon the seller's ignorance; which a glance at a diagram might have removed."* In LAND SURVEYING, nothing equals the chain in the field, for exciting the mind. Rules will always be sought with eagerness, when operations demand them.

112. LINEAR DRAWING is a branch of instruction to which a high degree of importance should be attached, both as a means of improving the perceptive powers, and as auxiliary to almost every branch of art. In schools for the poor, it ought on no account to be neglected. The best plan that can be pursued, probably is, to commence with simple geometrical lines and figures; then to make the pupil execute animals, or other objects; and then maps and charts. Further than this, you may not find it either practicable or desirable to go.

113. In the common schools of America, much importance is attached to the study of COMPOSITION. With us it has been almost entirely neglected. I suppose it has generally been imagined, that prejudice would be excited, by any attempt to teach the children of the poor to express their thoughts on paper. Under suitable regulations, however, this exercise might be rendered highly salutary, not only as a discipline of the mind, but as a means of moral improvement. Perhaps the best way of introducing such a practice is, for the teacher to read

* Machinery of Education, by the Rev. W. C. Woodbridge.

a short and striking narrative; requiring the pupils, first to listen attentively, and then to write upon their slates as much of it as they can in their own words. They might in this way be trained to habits of attention; and at the same time be tested as to their proficiency in writing, spelling, grammar, and the formation of sentences.

114. In all you do, however, remember that *The great object of your care should be to form* GOOD MENTAL HABITS; to accustom children to discern betwixt good and evil; and to teach them, not only how to acquire knowledge, but how to apply it. A mind may be filled with all the " knowledge and mysteries" of other men, but it is " poor and miserable" still, if it wants the judgment or the vigour, necessary to use its attainments with propriety and effect.

115. The habit, for instance, of attention to ABSOLUTE ACCURACY, is not merely important in the acquisition of knowledge; it has much to do with the happiness or misery of life. " How many of the most mischievous falsehoods and calumnies originate from the want of this habit! How often do suspicion, and jealousy, and coolness, and even enmity, originate in families and in society, simply from an inaccurate description or narrative! And how often is there reason to fear, that the innocent suffer, and the guilty escape, in our courts of justice, from similar causes! It will require but a little attention to the manner in which witnesses of

real honesty, and under the sanction of an oath, often give their testimony, and the totally new aspect which the narrative assumes, under the cross-examination of an acute advocate, to perceive the immense importance of cultivating a faculty on which the life of others often depends." *

116. Now, accuracy in statement, where there is no wish to deceive, depends entirely on the power of the MEMORY; and memory again depends on habits of attention: every pursuit, therefore, that tends to cultivate this faculty, should be regarded as valuable, not merely as affording additional *power* for acquiring knowledge, but also as determining character.

117. But ATTENTION, as every one knows, is very much influenced by habit; so much so, indeed, that processes, which in the first instance require the closest attention, are after a time performed without any effort whatever. This is illustrated every day, in the rapidity with which we combine columns of figures. In like manner, a person little accustomed to intellectual processes, advances step by step, with minute attention to each as he proceeds; while another perceives at once the result, with little consciousness of the steps by which he arrived at it. " For this reason it frequently happens, that in certain departments of science, the profound philosopher makes a bad teacher. He

* Sketches of Hofwyl.

proceeds too rapidly for his audience, and without sufficient attention to the intermediate steps by which it is necessary for them to advance; and they may derive much more instruction from an inferior man, whose mental process on the subject approaches more nearly to that which in the first instance must be theirs."* Habits of an opposite character, namely, of INATTENTION, are fatal to intellectual advancement. A mind of this description is worse trained than that of the savage, on whose accurate observation and powers of memory, the lives of travellers so often depend. I have myself been guided, more than once, through the intricacies of a South American forest, by a male or female Indian, under circumstances which obliged me to stake my safety altogether upon their habits of minute attention.

118. The influence of ASSOCIATION, both on the memory and on the general character, should also be borne in mind. Dr. Abercrombie refers our associations to three classes :—1. Natural or philosophical association. 2. Local or incidental association. 3. Arbitrary or fictitious association. "The principle on which they all depend," he says, "is simply the circumstance of two or more facts, thoughts, or events, being contemplated together by the mind, though many of them have no relation to each other except this conjunction."

---

* Abercrombie on the Intellectual Powers.

The associations referred to under the first head, arise out of " the *real* relation of facts to each other, or to subjects of thought previously existing in the mind." Those of the second are "formed according to no other relations than such as are entirely local or casual." The third are produced " by a voluntary effort of the mind; and the facts associated are not connected by any relation expect what arises out of this effort." The following example of natural or philosophical association is given as having occurred to himself:—

" In a party of gentlemen, the conversation turned on the warlike character of the Mahrattas, as compared with the natives of Lower India, and the explanation given of it by an author, who refers it to their use of animal food, from which the Hindoos are said to be prohibited by their religion. A doubt was started respecting the extent to which Hindoos are prohibited from the use of animal food; some were of one opinion, and some of another, and the point was left undecided. Reading, soon after, the Journal of Bishop Heber, I found it stated, that at one time during his journey, when a large supply of meat was brought to him, he ordered three lambs to be sent to his Hindoo attendants, and that the gift was received with every expression of gratitude. On another occasion such a fact might have been passed by without producing any impression; or it might have been slightly associated with the good bishop's attention to the comfort of all around him, but not remembered beyond the passing moment. In connexion with the discussion now mentioned, it became a fact of great interest, and never to be forgotten; and led to inquiry after more precise information on the subject to which it related.

" This trifling example may serve to illustrate the principle, that the remembrance of insulated facts does not depend merely upon the degree of attention directed to them, but also on the existence in the mind of subjects of thought with which the new fact may be associated. Other facts, as they occur, will afterwards be added, from time to time, giving rise to a progressive increase of knowledge, in a mind in which this mental process is regularly carried on. *This habit of attention and association ought therefore to be carefully cultivated,* as it must have a great influence on our progress in knowledge, and likewise on the formation of intellectual character, provided the associations be made upon sound principles, or according to the true and important relations of things. It is also closely connected with that activity of mind, which is ever on the alert for knowledge, from every source that comes within its reach; and that habit of reflection, which always connects with such facts the conclusions to which they lead, and the views which they tend to illustrate. On this principle also, every new fact which is acquired, or every new subject of thought which is brought before the mind, is not only valuable in itself, but also becomes the basis or nucleus of further information. Minds which are thus furnished with the requisite foundation of knowledge, and act uniformly upon these principles of enlarging it, will find interesting matter to be associated and remembered, where others find only amusement for a vacant hour, which passes away and is forgotten. There is also another respect in which the habit of correct and philosophical association assists the memory, and contributes to progress in knowledge; for by means of it, when applied to a great mass of facts relating to the same subject, we arrive at certain general facts, which represent a numerous body of the individuals, and the remembrance of which is equivalent to the remembrance of the whole."

119. The improvement of the JUDGMENT, or Reason, " that power by which we distinguish truth from falsehood, and combine means for the

attainment of our ends,"* should also be a primary object of concern. It is impossible for me here, to enlarge on the nature of this faculty, or even to refer to the various circumstances under which it is liable to become perverted or depraved. It is only necessary to observe, that it is guided by the same laws, when engaged in the investigation of truth, as when employed in the regulation of conduct; and consequently, is liable to be biased by personal feelings, and vitiated by immoral conduct. Young people should have their attention frequently directed to this truth; and while warned against being misled by fallacies, either in fact, in induction, or in argument, should especially be guarded against taking up opinions under the influence of interest or inclination, and yet giving themselves credit for unbiased inquiry. A few simple illustrations, exhibiting in various lights this sad propensity to self-deception, in relation to important truths, will satisfy an intelligent youth that he is *as responsible for his belief as for his conduct;* since he is answerable, not only for the faithful collection of facts and evidences, but for the temper of mind in which these evidences have been subsequently examined and weighed.

120. An ENLARGED COURSE of instruction, that which has reference to the general improvement and cultivation of the mind, as well as to the

---

* Stewart.

acquisition of diversified knowledge, is by far the best and *safest* that can be imparted to the children of the poor. It is true, they will in this case learn much that will be of no use whatever to them, so far as their *advancement* in life is concerned; much that will soon be forgotten; and much more that may never turn to account, in assisting them to obtain even those few necessaries of life, to the possession of which many of them must of necessity be limited. But why should this result be a source of regret? The chief *end* of knowledge is not to *get on* in the world; it is bad morality to inculcate such a notion: the end is rather to enable its possessor so to regulate the habits and business of life, that he may extract the greatest possible portion of comfort out of small means; and, by the cultivation of his intellectual faculties, be introduced to enjoyments of a higher and better order than those which lead in willing captivity the mass of the uneducated and the rude.

121. What particular branch of knowledge will be most valuable in future life to any given child, it is scarcely ever possible to predict. Circumstances, apparently the most trifling, often determine the settled pursuits of a long and active life. In the year 1828, a school was established, for three months only, among some of the Penobscot tribe of Indians, who reside on the Penobscot river. One of the pupils, Paul Joseph Osson, distinguished himself by unusual intelligence and proficiency.

After leaving the school, he returned for a year or two to his Indian habits and manners; but at the end of this time, being on a visit to Bangor, he happened to fix his eye upon some engravings in the shops, which made a very strong impression upon his mind. He was then taken to the room of a painter, and shown a considerable collection of portraits. From that time, painting seemed to take possession of his whole soul. He employed himself continually in sketching figures upon wood and bark, and commenced drawing and painting flowers, animals, miniature likenesses of his fellow Indians, and landscapes of considerable compass. He is now under regular tuition, and is said to be making respectable progress. It is related, that a lady, who was some years since visiting Old Town, the Indian village, was so struck with the fine figure and face of one of the Indian boys, that she sketched an outline of him on the spot: this made a strong impression on the boy, and on the tribe generally; and it is strongly suspected that Osson was the boy alluded to, and that this was the first spark of excitement that kindled his infant genius.*

122. In the great majority of cases, you cannot do more than impart to your pupils the simplest elements of knowledge. The children of the poor do not generally remain long enough at school to make any considerable advancement in learning.

* American Annals.

How important then is it, that you *let every branch receive attention only in proportion to its probable utility;* that you never indulge in *favourite pursuits,* to the exclusion or neglect of those which are more important to your scholars; and that you conscientiously determine, that the interests of the great majority shall never by you, (as they too frequently are by others,) be cruelly and wickedly sacrificed, to the vanity of displaying the attainments of a small and favoured few. Reading and spelling are surely of more importance to a poor child than grammar and geography; and arithmetic will be more valuable to him in life than a knowledge of history. If he cannot, therefore, attain all, there must be no question as to which shall be chosen. Each must receive attention according to its relative importance, whatever may happen to be your own peculiar predilections. Above all, let it be your grand object to teach every thing with eternity in view. That instruction is little worth, which does not embrace man's *whole* existence; and which has not as distinct a reference to the world that is to come, as to that which now obtrudes its claims with such unwarrantable importunity.

123. Here, however, let me warn you of the danger a teacher incurs by the too ready adoption of what he may consider NEW and IMPROVED METHODS of INSTRUCTION. Experiments are often valuable, but then they need to be made very cautiously;

a large number of facts and observations ought to be accumulated, before any practice involving material changes, is introduced into a school. On this subject I should recommend you to read the chapter on *Scheming*, in Mr. Abbott's Teacher. He very justly remarks, that " in almost all the cases where the wonderful effects of supposed improvements are hastily proclaimed, the secret of the success is, not that the teacher has discovered a *better* method than the ordinary one, but that he has discovered a *newer* one. The experiment will succeed in producing more successful results, just as long as the novelty of it continues to excite unusual interest and attention in the class, or the thought that it is a plan of the teacher's own invention, leads *him* to take a peculiar interest in it. And this may be a month, or perhaps a quarter, and precisely the same effects would have been produced if the whole process had been reversed."

124. The men who have really effected improvements in education, and left their mark on the rising generation, are very few. The three who of late years have attracted the greatest share of attention, are Pestalozzi, Fellenberg, and Jacotot. I cannot do more than briefly allude to these celebrated names; I must refer you to other sources, for extended information respecting their history and plans.

125. Henry Pestalozzi was born at Zurich, on the

12th of January, 1745. He was originally intended for the ministry; but after pursuing the usual course of studies, he resigned that profession, and turned his attention to the correction of what he conceived prevailing errors in the education of the young. His great object appears to have been, at once to improve the intellect and amend the heart, by imparting a knowledge of *things* rather than of words, and by exciting and developing benevolent affections. The great instrument he employed was *love*, and he appears to have possessed an amazing talent for so wielding that power, as to secure the most unbounded influence over the young. His long life was singularly chequered, and its end melancholy. He died in 1827, at the age of eighty years, overwhelmed with the disappointments and mortifications which he had in a great measure brought upon himself, by a too credulous reception of the extravagant flatteries of his disciples.

126. Emmanuel Fellenberg, who is a man of rank and fortune, is still living, and his institution at Hofwyl, about six miles from Berne, is an object of great interest to the philanthropist. The colony of Mey Kirk, at the distance of five or six miles, is a branch of the institution. It consists of eight or ten poor boys, who are placed under the direction of a teacher, on a spot of uncultivated ground, from which they are expected to obtain the means of subsistence. Hofwyl is in every respect a place

of *education*, of which the instruction imparted is only one means, and therefore *principles*, rather than *methods*, are to be gathered from its observation. The founder of Hofwyl proposes nothing less than " to develop all the faculties of our nature, physical, intellectual, and moral, and to endeavour to train and unite them into one harmonious system, which shall form the most perfect character of which the individual is susceptible, and thus prepare him for every period and every sphere of action to which he may be called." The *leading principles* of the institution are fully explained and illustrated in the delightful " Sketches," to which I have already several times referred; and so far as they can be made to apply to common day schools for the children of the poor, I have endeavoured to embody them in these letters.

127. M. Jacotot, who is, or was, professor of the French language at the university of Louvain, styles his system, " Universal Instruction and Intellectual Emancipation." A compendious exposition of the principles and practice of this teacher has recently been published, from which it appears, that the peculiarity of Jacotot's system consists in little more than the extensive, if not universal application of an old precept, " *Learn something thoroughly, and refer every thing else to it.*" His motto is, " Tout est en tout," which has been thus paraphrased: " Every thing is to be learnt thoroughly, and all possible use made of

facts already known, in order that they may be used as paths to lead the learner to regions *unknown* and still to be explored."* This principle is certainly good, whatever may be the character of Jacotot's application of it. The probability is, that he, like many other persons who attach themselves exclusively to one plan, knows his *idea* to be a good one, and so rides it to death.

128. Improvements in education, however, like improvements in every thing else, bring with them corresponding dangers; these sometimes arise (as in Jacotot's case) from pushing new plans and principles too far, and sometimes from an instructor working the additional power they give, with too high a pressure, upon minds predisposed to extraordinary intellectual activity.

129. Two very different classes of minds are exposed in opposite directions to danger, from the singular facilities which are now afforded for the acquisition of knowledge; I mean the indolent and the precocious. A mind that waits to be acted upon, instead of exerting its own native faculties, is not an improving mind. The aim of a good teacher is not so much to infuse knowledge, as to develop power—to encourage and to invigorate effort; he well knows, that the moment any mind begins to depend upon the facilities afforded it,

---

* Quarterly Journal of Education, vol. i. Review of Jacotot's system.

rather than upon itself, its efforts are impaired and its growth checked. The *easiest* way of learning a thing is not always the *best*. If all the truths of any science could be transferred in a moment to a learner's mind, without any exertion of his own, it would do him very little good; he would lose all the *benefit*, both of thinking and reasoning. It is far better that he should find the road somewhat rough, and be his own pioneer in clearing and levelling it.

130. But if it be (as it certainly is) an evil, to make the acquisition of knowledge *so* easy, that the mind becomes almost passive in its reception, and indolently ceases to make those efforts by which alone it can acquire strength and vigour, let it never be forgotten, that a far greater and more tremendous amount of mischief is accomplished, when, by undue excitement, an *excessive* intellectual development takes place, and the body, enfeebled by the dangerous activity of the brain, becomes the sport of a morbid irritability, or sinks into premature decay. Now, I think there are few *good* schools, where there is not some danger of one or more minds being injured in this way. The vanity of the parent, the ambition of the child, the pleasure which the teacher experiences, when he succeeds in exciting and developing one or more faculties to an extraordinary degree, all combine to promote that excessive intellectual activity, which is always perilous, and often fatal. I speak not

now of the *moral* effects of this unnatural excitement, how it enfeebles the will, how it excites the passions, and, by the increased susceptibility which it occasions, how it leads directly to excessive sensuality.* I say, I speak not *now* of these, because I am looking simply at its physical effects; and viewing the matter in this light alone, I am borne out by the united testimony of medical writers, in the assertion, that undue, and especially *premature* intellectual excitement, is the frequent, if not certain forerunner of impaired health, and of an early grave.

131. Take care then of precocious children; have no part in the process which is handing them over to disease and death. " The early history of the most distinguished men will, I believe, lead us to the conclusion, that early mental culture is not necessary, in order to produce the highest powers of mind. There is scarcely an instance of a great

---

* At Hofwyl, more than one instance has occurred, in which it was necessary to diminish the amount of a pupil's intellectual efforts, in consequence of the alarming tendency to sensuality which it produced. The same general truth is illustrated, by the comparison of nations and communities in different stages of civilization. While a certain degree of culture will diminish the sensuality of a savage tribe, or of a new colony, it rolls back in overwhelming waves upon those nations who have attained the height of cultivation and refinement, and whose intellectual faculties have been cultivated beyond the due proportion of their moral faculties.—*Woodbridge.*

man, one who has *accomplished* great results, and has obtained the gratitude of mankind, who in early life received an education in reference to the wonderful labours which he afterwards performed. Those men who have stamped their own characters upon the age in which they lived, or who, as Cousin says, have been the ' true representatives of the spirit and ideas of their time, have received no better education when young, than their associates, who were never known beyond their own neighbourhood.' " * Dr. Spurzheim says, " No school education, strictly speaking, ought to begin before seven years of age." But this opinion must be taken with limitations. Perhaps it would be better to say, that no intellectual *effort* ought to be required before that period. An infant school should be the happy asylum of babes, rescued by the hand of benevolence from penury, negligence, and vice: when such an institution becomes an " *intellectual hot-house*," it should be put down as a nuisance of the very worst description.

132. Do not then be found among those who foolishly complain that children are *childish*,—they ought to be so. The slower good fruit ripens, the better and the more valuable does it eventually become. The auto-biography of Zerah Colburn, the American youth, who, in the year 1812, was

---

* Brigham on the Influence of Mental Cultivation upon Health.

exhibited in London and Paris, and who, after astonishing the world by his power of calculation, and subsequently obtaining the best instruction, first in the college of Henry the Fourth at Paris, and afterwards, under the kind patronage of the Earl of Bristol, in Westminster school in London, has at length settled down into a useful, but not extraordinary Wesleyan preacher: his powers, it is said, greatly exhausted by undue exercise, and his mind, as a whole, enfeebled, rather than strengthened, by the original predominance of one faculty, affords an instructive lesson, not only to those who in his case cherished unwarrantable expectations, but to all, who in every place are idolizing a precocity, which, if rightly understood, would be the occasion of anxiety, rather than of joy.*

133. The bearing which some of the foregoing observations have on religious instruction, will not escape the notice of the judicious parent or Sunday

---

* It is well known to those who have been in the habit of visiting the Borough Road school, that in that establishment a class of boys are frequently brought out for inspection, who every day perform feats in mental arithmetic, far exceeding those which Bidder, a few years ago, excited so much notice by accomplishing. It may not be so well known, that so far from precocity of talent being cultivated there, these very boys, who exhibit such a remarkable aptitude for calculation, are on that account kept back from all excitements, and as much as possible employed in pursuits which require no effort of mind whatever.

school teacher. On this aspect of the subject, (precocity in religious knowledge,) I could say much, but I forbear; the ground is tender, and it is difficult to avoid misapprehension. It will be safer for me to express my sentiments in the language of another, than to clothe them in my own. I *adopt*, therefore, the words of a correspondent of the Christian Observer, and add, " Mental precocity is not a healthy attribute, even when it assumes the character of religion. The religion of little children ought eminently to be an affection of the heart, grounded indeed upon scriptural truth, the elements of which are intelligible to a little child, but not ramified into all the doctrinal discussions and mental developments which we sometimes survey with wonder. Theology, as a science, may be made as great a stimulant to the infant mind as baby novel reading; and the effect will too likely be, that the subsequent relaxation will be in proportion to the undue tension. Evelyn's child [whose remarkable history had formed the subject of a previous paper,] was not altogether simple; there was something of the artificial, that which was not natural in his years, mixed with his lovely character; and so far as this is indicated, it weakens our sympathy. When he asks, ' if he might pray with his hands *unjoined*,' he is altogether the child. His piety, his reverence for God, his tenderness of conscience, his willingness to bear inconvenience or pain, where duty requires it, are thus incidentally evinced; while his scruple is so full of sincerity, that we sympathise, while we smile at his simplicity. But when he deals in abstract truths, and lays down theological propositions, such as that 'all God's children must suffer affliction;' and when he declaims against the vanities of the world, before he had seen any; he is no longer a child of five years old speaking from his own simple feelings; he is either repeating by rote, or he has gained an early maturity of thought and an abstraction which are not natural, and are not of necessity religious. In giving up his own little world for God; in bearing with meekness the afflicting hand of his heavenly Father; in expressing his reverence, by wishing to assume the accustomed attitude of infantile devotion; and above all, in his simple and affecting prayer, 'Sweet Jesus, save me—deliver me—pardon my sins—let thine angels receive me;' he evidences an early growth of the *spiritual* affections: but in abstracting all this into theological propositions, he merely shows the prematurity of the *mental* powers, or more probably, what he had heard and remembered. ' My son, give me thy heart,' as distinct from the mere exercise of the understanding, is the command of our heavenly Father; and in the case of little children, and often of older converts, the heart may be far in advance of the intellect."

134. Before concluding this letter, which has already extended far beyond my original design, I feel it necessary to add a few words, on the extent

to which the *principles* laid down in it may be made applicable to *Sunday school* instruction. At present, (and I fear it will be the case for some years yet to come,) a large portion of the time and energy of Sunday school teachers is expended in the impartation of the elements of reading. Whatever, therefore, is adapted to facilitate this part of their labour, (and paragraphs 67 to 89 come under this description,) cannot be either unacceptable or inappropriate.

135. But I would not willingly be persuaded, that this is all the benefit that persons not professionally engaged in the work of tuition can reap from these hints on the " art of communicating knowledge." The enlarged and diligent study of the philosophy of teaching, by *all* classes of the community, would be a great public benefit. Whenever such a taste shall happily be excited, the Sunday school will be the first place in which its advantageous effects will be manifested. Then will the most accomplished minds be found foremost in this labour of love; and never till then, will the yet unsuspected power of the Sunday school, as an instrument of moral regeneration, be fully tested and developed.

LETTER VI. TO THE SAME.

REWARDS AND PUNISHMENTS.

136. " Experience," says Fellenberg, " has taught me, that *indolence* in young persons is so directly opposite to their natural disposition to activity, that, unless it is the consequence of bad education, it is almost invariably connected with some constitutional defect."* And yet, as every one knows, the professed object of more than one half the PUNISHMENT inflicted in schools is to compel application; while we are told on all hands, that without the constant stimulus of REWARD, it is impossible to secure any long-continued effort to excel.

137. If, however, Fellenberg is right, in supposing that stimulant is only needed in morbid cases, and I see no reason to distrust his authority, how important is it, that the greatest care should be exercised in correcting indolence or inattention,

---

* Sketches of Hofwyl. Letter xiii.

lest, in attempting to remove the immediate evil, we should induce others of greater magnitude, and inflict permanent injury on the character. It is always dangerous to *punish* children for idleness; the pain inflicted, instead of being regarded as an inconvenience resulting from a fault, is almost sure to be associated in the child's mind with the industry and learning which it is intended to promote. It is obvious that no association can be more mischievous.*

138. Rewards, if judiciously bestowed, may, on the contrary, be productive of much good. In private families, and in very small schools, the influence which is founded on affection for the

---

* " Punishment ought to be used to deter a child from doing evil, but it ought never to be used to induce it to do good. For instance, you see a child strike another,—punish the offender, and while he is suffering, he ascribes the pain to the blow which he had inflicted on his companion. You thus establish in his mind the association of necessary contiguity between the blow and the punishment; and this association will deter him from a repetition of the offence. But suppose it should be your desire that your child should do what is good,—suppose you wish that he should read a chapter in the Bible, and he refuse, you punish him,—you then associate the punishment with the Bible, and this association is attended with injurious results. In a few *morbid cases*, where the child cannot be aroused to intellectual activity, it may be necessary to inflict punishment for idleness; but such cases are rare, and when they do occur, it will be found that neglect in early education is closely connected with their existence."
—*Dr. Bryce of Belfast.*

teacher, is doubtless better adapted than any other to stimulate attention and to awaken effort. His smile, when thus valued, is by far the best reward. But, as I have said elsewhere, it is a fatal error to lay down plans for a day school of two hundred children, which are in fact only adapted to a very limited number of pupils, living beneath the roof of the instructor, and altogether under his control. I again repeat, it is impossible for you to act the parent to two or three hundred children, whom you see only for a few hours in the day, or to employ, in these circumstances, to any great extent, that kind of power which springs only from constant and familiar intercourse. Hence arises the necessity, in large schools at least, for that kind of stimulant, which although in some respects objectionable, is supplied by EMULATION and by REWARD.

139. I know it is a question with many, whether emulation ought, under any circumstances, to be used as a motive to induce the young to apply themselves to the acquisition of knowledge. Essays and papers innumerable have been written, to show that this principle is ranked by the apostle Paul with the " works of the flesh," and should therefore find no place in schools where the spirit of christianity is intended to be inculcated. These writers associate with the term, pride and vanity, hatred and envy, ambition and selfishness. Others, understanding by *emulation*, simply *the desire of surpassing*, and considering that in this primary

sense it has no moral character whatever, but is good or bad, according to the objects and motives with which it is associated, maintain that emulation is one of the most important springs of action, and ought on no account to be dispensed with. It is plain, that the whole controversy, so far as Scripture is concerned, turns on the meaning attached to the word.* I confess to a decided leaning towards the opinions of those who take the more favourable view. Bad as our nature is, I cannot

---

* The word ζηλος signifies any *fervid affection of the mind*. Such is the *generic* idea, and when specifically applied, it may mean any *earnestness* or *engagedness* in any pursuit. In the New Testament it is generally applied to designate *anger, warmth of feeling*, in the way of indignation; *e. g.* in Acts v. 17; xiii. 45; Rom. xiii. 13; 1 Cor. iii. 3. But sometimes it is employed in a *good* sense; *e. g.* John ii. 17, "the zeal" (ζηλος) "of thine house,"—*i.e.* zeal for the honour of thine house. And in a sense like this last named, we generally employ it in our own language.

In Gal. v. 20, it plainly designates a bad passion, which is reckoned among "the works of the flesh." But as it may also imply simple *earnestness*, or *engagedness*, *warmth of feeling* in a good cause, (as in John ii. 17,) nothing can be drawn from the use of this word which will cast light on the subject of *emulation*. In the like manner is the verb παραζηλόω employed. It is used as meaning *to excite to emulation*, in a good sense, in Rom. xi. 11—14, and perhaps in Rom. x. 19. It is employed in a bad sense in 1 Cor. x. 22. The word itself, therefore, can determine nothing. It is in its own proper nature, merely *generic*, meaning to *excite*, to *stir up*, so as to do either good or evil.—*Prof. Stuart.*

but think that there *is* such a thing as a generous rivalry. I know that it is no uncommon occurrence for well-matched competitors to be the dearest of friends; and though envy may sometimes be stirred up for a moment, in consequence of discomfiture, I cannot but think, that if the parties " strive lawfully," resentment, if at all excited in the vanquished, will be short-lived. That competition has an important use, in teaching children their *relative* powers, cannot, I think, be disputed. This species of self-knowledge, so valuable in future life, and which no books can teach, can be gathered only in the field of contest. That struggles of this character are necessarily connected with a selfish desire of personal distinction;—with comparisons flattering to self, and injurious to others;—with jealousy, envy, and ill-will;—I can by no means admit. At the same time, it is quite plain that great care should be taken not to push rivalry too far; that the desire of superiority should always be made subordinate to the cultivation of kind and generous feelings; and that the victor and the vanquished should both be made sensible, not only that distinctions of every kind are relative, but that intellectual superiority is only to be desired, in so far as it is associated with moral excellence.

140. In the bestowment of a REWARD, the great point to be kept in mind is, the production of right impressions on the mind of the child, as to the intent and object of the gift. It should be distinctly

understood, that it does not in any sense partake of the character of *a payment*. The gospel teaches all of us, that nothing we can do *merits* reward; and we must take care, by our practice as well as by our instructions, to inculcate the same truth. He who is accustomed to do right, in order that he may obtain gifts here or hereafter, is at best a mercenary; he who does so in order that he may obtain the praises of men, or secure the advancement of his own interests, is but the *slave* of *vanity* or *selfishness;* while he who pursues the same course, looking only for his reward in that self approbation and quiet complacency which are the result of conscious rectitude and supposed superiority, is the victim of a vice more terrible and destructive, when viewed in " the light of God's countenance," and in relation to man's highest and best interests, than it is possible for any human power rightly to estimate. The deity to whom this man offers sacrifice,—before whose altar his incense perpetually arises, and in whose smile he finds his continual happiness,—is none other than—himself. Finding his pleasures only in his own thoughts, he is obliged " to conceive himself what he is not, for who is pleased with what he is?" He is an idolater, whose guilt is aggravated by the absence even of a pretext, that his devotions are intended to terminate somewhere beyond the *immediate* object of his adorations. Dust and pollution is the sole and ultimate divinity of a self-complacent man; he cannot enter into the presence even of his Maker, without carrying along with him thoughts and feelings appropriate only to a self-existent and independent being.

141. I press these remarks on your attention, because I know that many *educators* imagine, that if they can repress the outbreakings of a spirit of rivalry and ambition, all is well; whereas it is quite possible, by the injudicious management of these outward manifestations of depravity, only to throw the disease within, and to aggravate far deadlier evils which may be raging there.

142. A reward *ought* to be regarded only as a pleasant memorial of a good deed; its legitimate object is, to keep in memory the approbation which a superior mind has accorded to certain conduct; and its chief value arises from the association which it creates, between that which is pleasant, and that which is good. Hence its pecuniary value is of comparatively little moment. " If rewards are given at all," says Mr. Hall of Andover, (to whose valuable lectures I have elsewhere referred,) " let them be *rewards of merit*,* and not rewards of intellectual capacity. The dull of apprehension are not to be punished for being so, neither do the more gifted merit praise for what they have received from the hand of God. And on the whole, I am

---

* By rewards of *merit*, I here understand Mr. Hall to mean, rewards of habitual industry, of regular exertion, of general good conduct in relation to the studies of the school; and not *moral conduct* of any kind.

inclined to believe that the safest way is to dispense with rewards altogether, when they cannot be equally offered to all." But why not be offered to all? Only make their value to consist in the associations gathered around them, rather than in their pecuniary cost, and there will be no difficulty in making them sufficiently numerous to excite the desire and to gratify the expectation of the largest number. In this case too, they may be given at comparatively short intervals, the importance of which will be well understood by those who know enough of human nature to estimate the length of a year in the apprehension of a child. If, in addition, care be taken to avoid the production of too high a degree of excitement, and too exclusive a desire for distinction; if children are taught, that goodness in itself is from its very nature, at all times and without any exception, beneficial, and vice as invariably injurious, I do not think that either the permission of emulation, or the bestowment of rewards, will render any child less susceptible to better influences, less alive to appeals simply made to the conscience and the affections, or less disposed to cultivate any branch of moral excellence.

143. Rewards, how well and wisely soever they may be bestowed, will not however prevent transgression. "Offences will come;" and punishment, in one form or other, must be inflicted. And here, the first and great object to be secured, is *the retrospective association of the pain inflicted with*

the previous fault. All punishment should be of this retrospective character; it should never be inflicted to *enforce* the repetition of a good action, but always to *prevent* the repetition of a bad one; and the association of pain with that which is wrong, and of pleasure with that which is right, should always be kept in mind as its great object and end.

144. (2.) *It should be serious.* Ineffectual punishment does positive harm. No chastisement is beneficial which does not humble the delinquent; cause him to fear " the rod;" and thus tend to prevent the repetition of the fault.

145. (3.) *It should be unmixed with personal feeling.* " The child should never imagine that his educator is influenced in his discipline by the same passions he himself feels."* Hence a teacher should never punish a child for personal disrespect; he cannot do so without making the child sensible of its own importance, or without appearing to be actuated by a spirit of vengeance. The petulance and insult of one so inferior should always be treated with pity rather than with anger. " The insolence which has its origin in vanity or pride, is not likely to be reformed by punishing the numerous petty offences to which it will give rise. Our attention and efforts must be directed to the false state of feeling which gives birth to them, if

* Fellenberg.

we would be successful in convincing the offender of his fault, and in leading to its correction."*

146. (4.) *The punishment should be proportioned to the guilt involved in the offence, and not to the amount of inconvenience occasioned by it.* If you allow yourself to punish children merely because they have occasioned you some loss or inconvenience, you will often treat them with gross injustice, and will as certainly lose all hold of their affections.

" Little Charlotte was going out into her father's orchard: it was full of violets. 'Oh,' cries Charlotte, full of joy, 'what beautiful little flowers! I will gather my apron full, and make a nosegay for mother.' She immediately knelt down, and with great industry gathered her apron full; then she seated herself under an apple-tree, and made a handsome nosegay. 'Here it is,' said she; 'now I will run and convey it to my dear mother. How she will be delighted to kiss me!' To increase the pleasure of her mother, she crept slily into the kitchen, took a china plate, put the nosegay on it, and went on a full leap down the stairs, to find her mother. But Charlotte stumbled, fell, and broke the china plate into a hundred pieces, and scattered her nosegay all around. Her mother, who was in the room near by, heard the noise, and immediately sprang to the door. When she saw the broken plate, she ran back, seized a rod, and without inquiring a word about the manner in which the plate was broken, came to the child. Terrified both by the fall and on account of the broken plate, and half dead with fear of the rod, little Charlotte could only ejaculate, 'Dear mother! dear mother!' But this was of no service to her. 'You naughty child,' said her mother, 'break a beautiful plate, will you?' and chastised

* Fellenberg.

her severely. This injustice alienated her affections, and she never again brought a nosegay to her mother."*

147. (5.) *Regard should be had to the physical condition of the culprit.* Fellenberg observes, "The *habit of wandering* from one subject to another, which so often gives rise to useless remonstrances, and still more useless punishments, as well as *impatience* and *irritability of temper*, are frequently connected with debility or disorder of the nervous system, and should be treated accordingly. The educator should especially avoid the use of all violent means, where *debility of body*, or an *unsound state of health*, gives rise to faults or habits; and above all, where the pupil himself is sensible of his error, and struggles against it. In such cases the teacher should, on the contrary, take the place of a friend, and proffer his aid, as to one in need of assistance, instead of assuming the attitude of a severe judge."

148. (6.) *Punishment is effectual in proportion to its* CERTAINTY, *not to its* SEVERITY. Severity may produce fear; but fear, while it is in many respects degrading and corrupting, never acts as a prevention to evil, except where it is accompanied by a firm conviction that punishment will inevitably follow the commission of a fault; and then it is the *certainty*, not the *severity* of the chastisement, which effects the end in view.

* Salzmann's Art of Miseducation. *How to make yourself odious to children.*

"During the wars in Flanders, in the reign of Queen Anne, when the Duke of Marlborough and Prince Eugene commanded the allied army, a soldier in the division of the latter was condemned to be hanged for marauding. The man happened to be a favourite with his officers, who took great pains to save his life, and for this purpose interceded with the prince, who positively refused to grant their request. They then applied to the Duke of Marlborough, begging his grace to interfere; he accordingly went to Prince Eugene, who said ' he never did, and never would, consent to the pardon of a marauder.' 'Why,' said the duke, 'at this rate we shall hang half the army; I pardon a great many.' 'That,' replied the prince, ' is the reason that so much mischief is done by your people, and that so many suffer for it: I never pardon any, and therefore there are very few to be punished in my department.' The duke still urged his request; on which the prince said, ' Let the matter be inquired into, and if your grace has not executed more than I have done, I will consent to the pardon of this fellow.' The proper inquiries were accordingly made, and the numbers turned out very highly in favour of Prince Eugene; on which he said to the duke, 'There, my lord, you see the benefit of example. You pardon *many*; I never pardon *one*; therefore *few* dare to offend, and of course but *few* suffer.'

"This is one among the many confirmations which might be adduced of the truth of Beccaria's remark, that a ' *less* punishment which is *certain,* will do more good than a *greater* which is *uncertain.*'"

149. Whether CORPORAL PUNISHMENTS can, under all circumstances, be dispensed with, is a question I am not prepared to answer. That children may, in almost every instance, be governed without them, is I think indisputable; but that there are no cases in which the infliction of bodily pain should be

resorted to, is an assertion I am not prepared to make. Fellenberg concedes in theory and practice, that corporal punishment is *occasionally*, though rarely necessary. He thinks that *serious faults*, which result from *violent passions*, should be repelled with corresponding force at the moment, in order that a deep impression of physical pain may be associated with them, and serve as a check when excitement of this kind begins anew. He considers also, that it is sometimes necessary to give a physical check of this kind, *as a counterpoise to strong propensities or long-established habits;* as a means of arousing the pupil from that drowsy irresolution which is frequently the greatest obstacle to reformation. At the same time, he strongly condemns those arbitrary and violent punishments which appear to have no other source than the will of the master, and too often seem dictated by his passions. These he considers the cause of serious injury to the *character*, although they may be effectual in repressing the *exterior defects* of the pupil. "They often afford him," he says, "a species of consolation, in the idea that his sufferings are excessive, or at least that they are the result of passions like his own. They thus arouse his courage and sense of justice, in opposition to his educators. They bring his better principles into conflict with an authority which he is bound to respect, and thus utterly derange his views and feelings as to right and wrong. They often *excite passions* incomparably worse than the fault they are designed to correct, and strengthen them by calling them frequently into exercise. When they exert an influence, they only accustom the pupil to act from the lowest motives, the fear of his fellow men and of physical pain, and thus debase, instead of elevating his character."*

150. Professor Pillans goes farther. He has written ably and eloquently against any kind of corporal punishment whatever, and (which is far more) has proved that he could do without it in the High school of Edinburgh. Mr. Wood, on the other hand, leans to the occasional use of the cane; regarding corporal punishment as an evil, the use of which is only to be justified by necessity. He thinks that in large establishments like the Sessional school, that necessity is fairly made out; and he is decidedly of opinion, that if entirely withdrawn, the directors of that institution would be compelled to have recourse to some substitute equally degrading and objectionable. He says, " Often have we seen the bringing out of a child to receive a single stripe on the hand, restore that order and attention which the young teachers and their assistants had been unable previously to procure." And he asks, " Is there really any other method by which the same important end could, with children of six or seven years, or even upwards, so expeditiously, so effec-

* Sketches of Hofwyl.

tually, and at the same time less objectionably, be attained?" I think there is not; and therefore, much as I dislike the application of *force*, under any circumstances, I could not, as the director of a public school, insist upon its entire abolition.

151. Allow me now to offer two or three observations in relation to the general subject. 1. *Be slow to punish in any way.* Never be in haste to believe that a pupil has done wrong. Make every inquiry for evidence, and always try to establish the innocence of the accused party. If acquitted by the evidence adduced in his favour, he will love his teacher the better for having pursued this course; and if proved guilty, he will be more likely to be affected by what you may say to him.

152. (2.) *In rebuking sin, avoid alike the language and tones of execration and of indifference.* It is never well to make the worst of any occurrence. Calm and temperate remarks, offered in a serious spirit, are most likely to affect the heart and to awaken the conscience.

153. (3.) Never have a *punishing hour.* Except in special cases, it is far better for discipline to be exercised without attracting public notice. If every case of disobedience, or idleness, or disorder, is to be brought forward at a stated hour, and punishment inflicted in the presence of all, what other result can be expected, than that unpleasant associations will be formed, in connexion both with the school and the teacher,—and that, hardened by the

spectacle, the scholars will care little about sharing in a species of disgrace, with which their minds are so constantly familiarized? Sometimes, however, marking out an offence by inflicting punishment on the offender before the whole school, may be highly impressive. In a case of this kind, as a rare occurrence, it is desirable briefly to address both the transgressor and his schoolfellows, setting forth the act of punishment before all as a disagreeable necessity, arising out of the misconduct of the boy,—an evil inflicted much against the teacher's will. If this be the *true* state of the educator's feelings, the children will not fail to perceive it, and will be affected accordingly.

154. (4.) *Never delegate punishment, nor ever inflict it as the delegate of others.* It is an every day occurrence in many schools, for parents to come to the teacher, with earnest requests that he will severely punish their boy for misconduct at home,—and, strange to say, there are some teachers who are willing to be made in this way the object of the child's aversion and hate. Others again, with equal folly, are accustomed, in order to avoid the trouble and disagreeableness of correction, to request the parent to inflict at home, punishment for offences committed at school. The evils which invariably arise out of such monstrous improprieties are so obvious, that after what I have already said on the subject, it is, I trust, scarcely necessary to

guard you against a practice so absurd and mischievous.

155. The following general principles, translated from the German of Denzel, one of the most able living writers on this subject, will suitably conclude the few hints I have now offered for your consideration.

" In the application of rewards and punishments," he observes, " the educator will do well to observe the following suggestions:

" I. Since that which is good and right ought to be done because it is good and right, without reference to reward or punishment, it follows that neither rewards nor punishments are ever to be employed, so long as other means are sufficient to enable the educator to keep his pupils in the way of their duty.

" II. In his whole course of education and instruction, the teacher should exhibit such inducements to obedience, activity, exercise of talent, and love of order, as will in a great measure *remove the occasion of transgressing his commands*, and of the consequent punishment; and let obedience and learning carry with them their own reward.

" III. It is only merit, diligence, acquisition by close application, and not talents and particular gifts of nature, that can justify any claims to reward. In no case ought the effects of incapacity or of innocent weakness to be punished. It is merely neglect, levity, and indolence, with the effects of a perverted will, that are punishable.

" IV. Rewards should only please, excite, and animate; without producing by any means, vanity, pride, and haughtiness. In the same manner, punishments ought to be such as to awaken a desire for that which is good; they should warn and restrain from evil, and not produce in the child any distrust in his own powers. Rewards should never appear to be distinctions; and punishments should be considered as evils inflicted out of necessity, and not of choice.

" V. Rewards and punishments should be only sparingly applied, or they lose their beneficial influence. By their frequent use, the mind either becomes insensible to their influence, or it obtains an erroneous impression, that mankind in all their actions are to be influenced only by that which is to them personally profitable or injurious.

" VI. The more sensual the man is, and the more he lives merely for the present and for himself, and the younger he is, so much the sooner after the act must reward or punishment be applied. On the contrary, the older the child, the more he must be accustomed to expect his reward or punishment at a distance, and the more must he be taught to hope or fear the remote consequences.

" VII. Rewards and punishments should never be applied by the educator till after he has fully weighed the circumstances in a dispassionate state of mind, with perfect impartiality. Every indiscretion, every mistake in the circumstances, every perceptible favouritism for an individual, effaces from the heart of the child whatever is beneficial in reward or punishment; that is, the sense of its necessity and propriety. The passionate man always commits errors. He mistakes the good, or overvalues it in his reward. That which is wrong is equally misunderstood, and attributed to the worst motives, and punished with excessive severity. Punishment should never be applied in anger, and still less with a sneer, or scorn, or an air of triumph; but rather always with marks of compassion for the child. Children should feel that the educator is compelled to the measure, and that it is disagreeable to him. When he imprudently punishes, he necessarily alienates the hearts of his pupils, and fosters a refractory, turbulent disposition; but when punishment is properly applied, it leaves a permanently good impression, and the educator is esteemed and beloved as a father. For a general rule, the approbation of the teacher is a sufficient reward for all *moral conduct*. In no case should it be encouraged by a determined precise premium. No rewards are proper in the religious part of education; for they might lead to the opinion that mankind could merit the favour of their God by their good works."

LETTER VII. TO THE SAME.

MORAL AND RELIGIOUS INFLUENCE.

156. It has been beautifully said, that " TRUTH, considered in itself, and in the effects natural to it, may be conceived of as a gentle spring or water-source, warm from the genial earth, and breathing up into the snow-drift that is piled over and around its outlet. It turns the obstacle into its own form and character, and as it makes its way increases its stream; and should it be arrested in its course by a chilling season, it suffers delay, not loss, and waits only for a change in the wind to awaken and again roll onwards." *

157. So would I describe the present relative position of knowledge and religion. The scattering abroad of knowledge, and the general diffusion of the elements of science among the people, may, for a time, like the snow-drift which covers the fountain, appear to impede, rather than advance the triumphs of the gospel; but it is in truth only destined to

* S. T. Coleridge.

accelerate its progress. The quiet, but insinuating master influence beneath, is silently gathering strength from the apparent hinderance, and preparing to break forth afresh with the force and volume of a torrent.

158. Many amiable and excellent persons are slow to perceive this; they are hard to be persuaded, that whatever is gained for knowledge must eventually be gained for christianity; and they tremble, at the very moment when the dictates of faith and reason alike call upon them to rejoice. Hence it happens, that while many, influenced by selfishness and pride, openly mourn over " the emancipation of the human reason from a legion of devils," because it involves " the loss of a herd of swine;" others, from whom better things might have been expected, stand by unconcerned, as this great work of humanity and religion falters in its course, or at best, urges its way by slow and painful steps. I trust it is scarcely necessary to say to you, *Sedulously avoid this mischievous error.*

159. Never give place for a moment to the idea, that intellectual advancement is in any degree unfavourable to moral improvement, or imagine that you will be more likely to promote true christianity by *exclusive* attention to religious instruction. While you are deeply anxious that all you teach should be based upon the gospel, and sanctified by the Holy Spirit, never forget that children have duties to perform in this world as well as the next, and

that it is cruelty, as well as folly, to deprive them of any natural right, under the pretext of extraordinary care for their spiritual interests. Rightly understood, the two invariably coincide: the enlargement of the intellect is favourable to the improvement of the heart;* " reason" is " assisted by faith," and " taste" is " purified by devotion." Keeping this cautionary remark in view, I may now venture to say, " Gird up the loins of your mind," and bend your undivided energies to the accomplishment of the great ultimate object of all your labours—the production of good moral and religious influences.

160. And here allow me to offer you one word of preliminary advice. It is this:—*Take rational and scriptural views, of the nature of the Being on which your influence is to be exerted.* If you set out with the idea, that the heart of a child is a fountain of love and purity,—that its affections, untainted by evil, will naturally gush forth towards the good and the beautiful, when presented to its notice,—that its mind is a white and pure tablet, on which you may inscribe what you will;—I say, if, instead of listening to the voice of scripture and of reason, you take up with these miserable sentimentalities, your disappointment is sure to be both

---

* The committee of the general assembly of the church of Scotland, state in their report on schools in the Highlands, that *those in which the greatest variety of secular instruction is imparted, are most distinguished by a religious character.*

bitter and complete. Rest assured, that " folly is bound up in the heart," even " of a child," and regulate your expectations accordingly.

161. Against an opposite error, that of supposing (as some do) that since God alone can change the heart, the improvement of the natural dispositions is altogether out of our reach, I trust you need scarcely be warned. This is a monstrous presumption, and can never be too severely reprobated. All experience—the history of the church in all ages—goes to prove, that while at various periods, the world has been startled and instructed by the sudden and permanent conversion of large numbers of the profligate and the profane,—the " salt of the earth," the benefactors of the world, whether considered individually or in the aggregate, have generally been gathered from the habitations of the amiable, the intelligent, and the devout.

162. In moral education, a twofold work has to be accomplished: " the faculty of reason must be taught how to judge rightly between truth and error, good and evil;"* and *the habit of acting* rightly must be formed, in order that the imagination, the passions, and the affections, may be accustomed to bow to the decisions of reason, when thus enlightened and strengthened. The first of these, (the formation of right judgments,) has long been a primary object of our efforts; the last,

* Hooker.

(the formation of habits and the regulation of emotions,) has not yet received that share of attention which its paramount importance demands. It may be worth inquiry, whether more cannot be done in this way than has hitherto been considered practicable.

163. To accomplish any good at all, however, remember, *the affections of your pupils must be secured.* If they do not love you, they will repel all your attempts to do them good. There must be sympathy between you and them, or all your efforts to influence them will be vain. Your first step, therefore, must be, to *secure a place in their most agreeable associations.* When your presence and society is a source of joy, it may easily be made the occasion of benefit. I have already said so much on the art of obtaining influence, (Letter III.) that I need scarcely add, *It will not be gained by indulgence.* Mr. Abbott has truly said, " It is one of the mysteries of human nature, that indulgence never awakens gratitude or love in the heart of a child." Firmness regulated by kindness,—a kindness not only felt, but expressed in acts of sympathy and love,—will alone secure any efficient hold on the affections of the young.

164. I would here, however, again request you to bear in mind, that the kind of influence which the teacher of an elementary school can exercise over his pupils, is in many respects very different from that which can be brought to bear by a wise

parent or tutor. It must be, as I have before said, influence exerted for the most part, not on the individual, but on the mass, and consequently, to a great extent, through the agency of general arrangements, rather than of personal intercourse. If particular children are selected, as the occasional companions of the teacher out of school-hours, (and this is highly desirable,) the favoured few, thus brought into a closer and more intimate fellowship with himself, must, on this principle, be instructed, not so much with a view to their individual benefit, as that from them may go forth an influence, which shall extend itself over the little community in which they dwell.

165. But to proceed. In all attempts to exercise moral influence over the young, *the faithful inculcation of Divine Truth from the Bible is the first point to be regarded.* To enlarge upon the excellency of scripture, or to show its adaptation to all the wants of humanity, is here, I trust, unnecessary. Were the book the production of man only, unassisted by inspiration,—did it carry with it no rebuke,—did it leave sin untouched,— would it but cease to be an accuser, or agree to descend from the judgment-seat, we cannot for a moment doubt that, containing, as Sir William Jones has well said it does, " more true sublimity, more exquisite beauty, purer morality, more important history, and finer strains, both of poetry and eloquence, than could be collected within the

same compass from all other books which were ever composed in any age or in any idiom,"—it would at once push aside all competitors, and be extensively and anxiously incorporated into the whole system of education, as the foundation and cornerstone of all improvement. Why it does not occupy such a place we all know too well.*

166. I should say then, first of all, if it be possible, *let every child have, every day, some portion of Divine Truth, however small, stored up in its understanding and memory.* It is the *reiteration*, day after day, of truth upon the mind, that makes the impression. To be remembered, however, it must interest; and to interest, it must be understood. To effect this purpose, the catechetical form

---

* Fellenberg's observations on this subject are striking; and as coming from him, they may have weight in quarters where scarcely any other individual would be heard. He says, " We see in *our days*, that *every thing* which *parents*, which *nature*, which *conscience*, and the observation of our own hearts can accomplish, for the moral development of children, is *inadequate*. Let this (the Old Testament) be the first history presented to the child, and let him be deeply imbued with the spirit of the Bible." Of himself he says, " We establish our institutions upon the basis of genuine christianity. We proceed, in the commencement of our labours, upon the essential principles and conditions of the gospel. The best practical example for the educator is to be found in the Saviour of men; and in the result we should aim at no other object, than the realization of that kingdom of God to which he has directed mankind."

of instruction, which, as Dr. Johnson well defines it, is simply " asking questions, and correcting the answers," will doubtless be found in general the most appropriate. The practice of reading from a book a certain number of prescribed questions, and hearing the child repeat by rote the words which are set down for him as the answers, is, in my opinion, of little value. I may be wrong,—many wise and good men differ from me on this point; but in my view, no catechetical instruction is worthy the name, in which the answer given by the child does not suggest the succeeding question.

167. Illustrations of an interesting character from " the world without," should at all times be anxiously sought. Such a text, for instance, as Jer. viii. 7, might very properly introduce a brief account of the habits and migration of birds. Where is the child who would not receive a deeper impression from the lesson it conveys, by associating with it his first acquaintance with the departure of the swallow on the approach of winter? In like manner, Eccl. i. 7, would seem *naturally* to lead you to explain the evaporation which is constantly taking place from the surface of the deep;—how it is, that notwithstanding all the waters of the Nile, the Po, the Rhone, the Ebro, the Danube, the Nieper, and the Don, pour themselves incessantly into the Mediterranean sea, it still does not increase in size. You will soon see how deep an interest will be excited, on finding the

explanation of the whole matter in this single text: "Unto the place from whence the rivers come, thither they return again." The formation of coralline rocks and islands, is another remarkable phenomenon, which may be made forcibly to illustrate Divine truth. The minuteness of the insect, and the gigantic character of the work it performs, strikingly teach how weak and humble is the instrumentality by which God often accomplishes his mightiest purposes. In this way the agreement which subsists between nature and revelation might be strongly impressed.

168. (2.) *Carefully ascertain, at an early period, that the elementary truths of the christian faith are understood and firmly rooted in the mind.* Allow me strongly to impress attention to this point, for it is very often grievously neglected. By the elementary truths of revelation, I mean such as relate to the being and attributes of God, the immortality of the soul, and a state of future retribution; and I venture to say, without fear of contradiction, that it is not an uncommon thing to find children professedly acquainted with the facts and doctrines of the Bible, long before they have any clear conceptions on these, "the first principles of the gospel of Christ." Can we wonder, that a structure so hastily reared, is in future life so easily undermined and destroyed? I attribute a great deal of prevailing infidelity, (especially among those who have received what is called a religious

education,) to this ill-judged practice of building up in the understanding a dogmatical system of theological truths, without first even attempting to lay a firm foundation in this broad ground-work of Divine revelation.

169. It is by no means necessary to go through any process of reasoning, to convince a child of the being of a God. The conviction that every effect must have an adequate cause is intuitive. The child recognizes and acts upon convictions of this character every day. If it handles a curiously constructed toy, it intuitively infers a skilful maker; and if it sees a house, it as certainly infers that the skill and labour of many have been engaged in its erection. The simplest step in reasoning imaginable, in like manner, leads from the creature to the Creator. Power, wisdom, and goodness, are inscribed upon every field and flower, and legible in every arrangement which has been made for the provision, whether of man or beast; but thoughtlessness and inattention detect no beauty, and discover no excellence. To remedy this, the mind should be accustomed, from a very early period, to mark the unerring skill and profound wisdom with which the most ordinary operations of the Divine hand are conducted; to associate in all its investigations the books of nature and of revelation; and invariably to connect the observation of the one, with the instructions and explanations of the other.

170. Sometimes it may be well to select an *extraordinary* instance of fertility or of beauty, and to make this the ground-work of useful remark. The fact, for instance, that a single grain of wheat has been known to produce 7455 other grains; or that one dwarf pea has proved the parent of above 500 peas; or that a single peach-tree has produced 1560 fine peaches;* might be made, in the hands of a wise teacher, to illustrate in the most interesting manner the bounteousness with which God supplies us, not only with the necessaries, but with the luxuries of life. It is highly important that the children of the labouring classes of society, in the midst of their many trials and difficulties, should be accustomed to take affectionate views of that divine and blessed Being, whose " tender mercies are over all his works."

171. The doctrine of the immortality of the soul, may seem at first sight to be much more difficult to explain to a child; but Mr. Gallaudet, in his " Child's Book on the Soul," has shewn, that even this may very easily be brought within infantile comprehension. He suggests, that a child should first be led to compare successively the properties of a pebble, a flower, a watch, an animal, and a human being. " In each object," he observes, " the pupil discovers some qualities which belonged to the preceding, with some new ones; and on arriving

* Turner's Sacred History.—Notes.

at the human being, he perceives that it has *life, movements, powers*, which neither the flower, nor the watch, nor the animal possesses; that we have *something*, of whose existence we are conscious, of whose *power* we have constant evidence, but of whose *nature* all the researches of metaphysics have informed us only of its negative properties."* He may then be taught, that it is this *something* which must *live for ever*. One remark of Mr. Gallaudet's is too valuable to be omitted,—it is this: " If inquiries are made, or difficulties started, let them be treated with the greatest attention. *They who would teach children well, must first learn a great deal from them.*"

172. To impress the doctrine of future retribution, and to prevent in mature life that " making free with Divine goodness," which leads so many to contemplate God exclusively under one aspect, and hence to conclude that he is characterised by " a bare single disposition to produce happiness," what can be better than the striking illustrations of the government of God, especially by punishments, which are found in the 2nd chapter of Bishop Butler's Analogy? I mention this book because it is generally accessible, and, with some exceptions, as simple as it is profound.

173. (3.) *Be unceasing in your endeavours to bring the word of God into contact with the*

---

* Woodbridge on Gallaudet.

conscience. Conscience is " the candle of the Lord, shining in the innermost parts of the body." Press truth then into its presence, with hope and vigour. Appeal frequently to this " light within," dim and flickering as it may be. You do much for your pupil, if you only keep alive the simple elementary idea, that there is ONE, whose sight he cannot escape, whose power he cannot resist, and that this wondrous Being, of whose greatness and majesty he has so many proofs, is ever appealing, by " a still small voice," to his convictions and affections, though he be but a little child. It is only by this constant reference to HIM, who " seeth not as man seeth," that you can ever hope to direct attention to the spirit and motive of conduct, or turn the mind from " man," who " looketh on the outward appearance," to the Lord, " who looketh on the heart."

174. *In all applications of scripture, however, be careful to choose your opportunity wisely.* There are periods when serious injury is done by urging the claims of religion. Never do so, for instance, when a child is under the influence of anger. To be scolded or lectured at such times from the Bible, can only produce disgust. The child associates the book with the idea of punishment, and probably looks upon it only as an instrument of wrath, wielded by you for the purpose of maintaining authority. Any period of strong emotion, of whatever kind, is indeed unsuitable. The heart must be tranquil,

and at rest, or valuable impressions are not likely to be produced.

175. *In the inculcation of scripture doctrines, be regulated by the age and capacity of those whom you have to instruct.* In this respect let Christ himself be your example. There were many truths which he kept back, only because his disciples were " not able to bear them;" and every judicious instructor must do the same. It is very painful to see, as we do sometimes, mere babes in years, as well as in knowledge, crammed with the " strong meat," instead of being fed with the " milk" of the gospel. Such a practice is every way pernicious. It is going back, to say the least of it, to the old and mischievous practice of repeating by rote, and it may be doing serious mischief. Theological *prating* has a dreadful tendency to harden the heart, and to deaden the sensibilities of the soul. We can never guard too carefully against the danger of instructing the tongue to outrun the heart. This abuse of doctrinal truth, be it remembered however, forms no argument at all against the judicious inculcation of " the whole counsel of God." If this be neglected, the morals even of the Bible will be found to have little power over the character in the hour of temptation. " Man wants power as much as direction; his hopes and his fears are the sinews of his virtue; and when even his mind is instructed, he is motionless towards

that which is right, until he feels the life of *love*. "We love him because he first loved us." Here is the spring of morality; the heart of the whole system of christian morals is the love of Christ. No education is religious, in any christian sense, without the knowledge of the gospel; and the hope of its practical influence rests, therefore, on the careful and full communication of its leading doctrines. To take the morals of the New Testament, and to discard its faith, is to sever the tree from the root while it is yet in bloom. The hues may be admired, and the fragrance be for a time, as "*a field which the Lord hath blessed;*" but "*their blossom shall go up as dust, because they have cast away the law of the Lord of hosts, and despised the word of the Holy One of Israel.*"*

176. If on these principles scriptural instruction be faithfully imparted, the accomplishment of one great object in education, the formation of A CORRECT MORAL TASTE, may, I trust, reasonably be expected. The next step is to seek the formation of RIGHT HABITS, the "masters of action," the "links" which, following each other " in the chain of custom," so often bind and enslave the soul. I shall mention a few of these, in the order in which they occur to my own mind, without giving any opinion as to their *relative* importance.

177. (1.) CLEANLINESS. The importance of physical

---

* Richard Watson's Sermon on Religious Education.

cleanliness,—its influence on the health and comfort of a school,—its connexion with taste and order,—and above all, its MORAL advantages, are so obvious, that it is unnecessary even to name them. No excuse should be taken for dirt; a rule which is of more importance, because, among the poor, cleanliness cannot always be maintained without unremitted and painful exertions. Let every child see, then, that you duly appreciate clean hands and a clean face; and reward attention to these points, by committing to such as are distinguished for this kind of excellence, some little charge, which will occasion their " light" to " shine" before their fellows, and thus contribute to form the same habits in those around them.

178. The great object of the teacher must always be, to *unite pleasant associations with what is right, and painful associations with what is wrong.* Habits are but repeated acts; whatever, therefore, tends to induce the *repetition* of a good act, and to *prevent* the repetition of a bad one, should be secured on the side of virtue. In the first instance, AUTHORITY must be put forth; after this, EXAMPLE will probably suffice. But a time comes when authority must cease, and example be withdrawn. In the absence of sound christian principles, nothing then is so powerful as ASSOCIATION. If, for any length of time, pleasure has been associated with the performance of duty, and pain with its neglect, there is every reason to hope that the bias of the

will may generally be determined in favour of that which is right.

179. A variety of means may be adopted to secure the desired result. A country schoolmaster, trained in the normal school of the British and Foreign School Society, was much grieved by observing a want of neatness and cleanliness in his monitors. He had long deplored this evil, without being able to remedy it, until it struck him, that he might effect his object, by gaining the confidence of the parents of those boys whose appearance he was desirous of seeing improved. He visited them several times before he ventured to touch upon the topic which occupied his attention. He then selected the most respectable and neatly dressed boy as his pattern. The dress of this boy happened to be a full and well made brown holland pinafore, surmounted by a neatly turned down linen collar. He set himself to work to estimate the cost of these articles, and the probable saving that might be effected in clothing already worn; and having completed his calculation, he put it so clearly before the parents, that, with the influence he had otherwise been able to gain over them, they were induced to accede to his wishes; and it is pleasing to know that these boys, to the number of about a dozen, have been supplied with a clean dress of this description ever since.*

* The plan of this little book does not admit of any extended remarks on physical education. I may, however,

180. (2.) SELF-DENIAL, as opposed to all greediness and gluttony, and to the indulgence of the lower appetites in general, is a duty you should invariably and anxiously inculcate. The influence which habits of this kind exercise over the future character and happiness of the man, is frequently overpowering. The French express in a precept of three words, "*Vivre de peu*,"* the great secret of independence. But this first of blessings can never be attained by one who is a slave of the lowest of all appetites, the love of eating and drinking. Now a child may soon be made sensible of this. He has probably felt too severely the inconveniences to which poor families are subject from such indulgences, to need much other proof of its evil tendency; but he is himself insensibly forming a similar taste. Warn him then of the first steps in this career of degradation; guard him against seeking enjoyment in any form of sensual indulgence whatever. Never give him any reward of this low character; and seize every opportunity to excite better feelings, by bringing under his notice, eminent instances of moral feeling triumph-

---

take this opportunity of strongly recommending a work lately published by Dr. Hodgkin, entitled, "Lectures on the Means of Promoting and Preserving Health." The price is moderate, and no school library should be without it. It is full of valuable information, and is particularly adapted to those who have the care of the young.

* "To live upon little."

ing over the strongest appetites. Sir Philip Sidney, at the battle of Zutphen, sending away untasted the cup of water; and David pouring out before the Lord, the precious draught, for which his soul had just before so intensely longed, are two examples which might in this way be turned to good account.

181. The evils and sorrows which INTEMPERANCE brings in its train, are so obviously connected with, and occasioned by sinful indulgence, that a better opportunity cannot probably be found, than that which a warning against this vice affords, to show how, in the providence of God, the pain connected with an evil action always arises out of itself. It is important that the young should be made to perceive, that the connexion which subsists between sin and pain, virtue and happiness, is not arbitrary, but necessary. The practice of using intoxicating liquors, as marks of courtesy and kindness, ought to be resolutely discountenanced. It leads directly to habits of inebriety, and by direct consequence, to the extinction alike of intellect and piety.

182. ECONOMY, as connected with habits of frugality and self-denial, may also, under judicious management, be cultivated with success. In some of our schools, SAVINGS BANKS have been established, and are found to prosper. I have received the following account of one o these institutions.

" A friend having stated, at one of our teachers' associations, that he had succeeded in establishing a savings bank, in connexion with his school, I immediately determined to make a similar attempt. My first intention was to invest the money in our local savings bank; but upon mentioning the subject to a gentleman connected with the school, who has kindly patronized every effort that I have made to promote the welfare of my boys, he represented to me the difficulties I might probably experience, in attending at the particular time and place, and otherwise acting in conformity with the rules of that establishment; at the same time offering to receive the savings of the children himself; promising to allow them the same interest as they would gain by depositing them in the bank, with the additional advantage, that every *shilling* should bear interest, whereas no interest is given by those institutions for sums under *fifteen shillings*. I need not say that I thankfully accepted his offer; and notwithstanding the poverty of the parents, and the sickness of the children, owing to the severity and dampness of the season, the deposits have amounted, on an average, to 13s. 10½d. per month, in a very small school. This money would, I am persuaded, have been expended in trash, had not a scheme been devised to prevent it. I may be allowed to remark, that if any gentleman can be found, as in this case, in whom the parents of the children have confidence, such an investment of the money is preferable to the ordinary savings bank. But this is by no means an essential point, for my friend and fellow teacher has proved the latter to answer every purpose, and has met with uniform kindness from its officers, who have declared, that to them, small sums are the most profitable deposits that are made.

" I receive the money at the opening of the school, in any sums that the children can bring, entering them at the same time in a book kept for the purpose; the several deposits are cast up on the first day of every month, and the amount paid into the hands of the gentleman before referred to, each child being presented with a ticket, on which is shewn the amount of his deposits for the month."

183. (3.) GENTLENESS. The labouring classes of England have long and justly been reproached by all foreigners, for their rudeness and incivility. No Englishman, indeed, who has travelled on the continent of Europe, unless utterly blinded by national prejudice, can fail to have observed the superior civilization and politeness of the peasantry of other countries, as distinguished from his own. Now, although it is quite true, that a rough, and even a rude exterior, may, and frequently does, consist with much real kindness of heart; and although it is equally certain, that polished manners are too often only a cloak for the indulgence of the most unbounded selfishness; it still holds good, that politeness is the legitimate representative of benevolence, and rudeness the spontaneous fruit of selfish unconcern for the interests and feelings of others. As such, therefore, without doubt, the one should be cherished, and the other shunned.

184. With this general object in view, then, *Repress in every instance the first indications of an unfeeling disposition, especially when manifested towards insects or dumb animals.* Captain Back, in his recent narrative of the expedition in search of Ross and his companions, mentions, with a frankness very honourable to himself, a little incident, which shows what a powerful influence a humane regard for the *life*, even of the most insignificant insect, will sometimes exercise. The party had encamped for the night on a spot where they

were tormented by mosquitoes. To get rid of the painful nuisance, Captain Back filled his tent with smoke, and then swept the stupified insects out at the door. It was observed that this procedure excited surprise; and he was soon after asked by one of the Indians, why he did not act as the great captain (Sir J. Franklin) had done? who, it seems, in the overflowing kindness of his heart, had been accustomed to say, when tormented by the flies, as he shook them off, " Let them live,—there's room enough in the world for us all." This regard for life had evidently made a deep impression upon these wild sons of the forest, and had excited thoughts and feelings which no exhortations whatever could have awakened. Now remember, that in this, as well as in many other particulars, your own example will occupy, in relation to the child, precisely the same position which that of the great captain did in relation to the savage.

185. Children, and all untutored persons, soon catch the spirit and imitate the actions of those with whom they associate, and to whom they look up as superiors; hence, the importance of always acting on the principle, that it is better to *endure* pain than to *inflict* it; ever remembering, that to cultivate and to exercise a spirit of kindness and of love, is *the great duty* impressed in every page of scripture, and continually enforced by the example of the Redeemer. The occasional introduction before the whole school, of an anecdote or story,

descriptive of the affection and tenderness frequently exhibited by animals towards each other, and especially towards their young, might be productive of the best effects. I append one as a specimen, in the form of a note.* Take care, however, not to spoil such a story by comments and reflections of your own. Children are in the practice of moralizing daily on the most common occurrences of life, and are much more likely to do so on a narrative of this description, if left to themselves.

186. A great point is gained, when young people are made to feel, that *no living thing is to be*

---

* " When the Carcasse frigate was locked in the northern ice, a she-bear and her two cubs, nearly as large as herself, came toward them. The crew threw to them great lumps of sea-horse blubber. The old bear fetched them away singly, and divided them between her young ones, reserving but a small piece for herself. The sailors shot the cubs, as she was conveying the last portion, and wounded her. She could just crawl with it to them, tore it in pieces, and laid it before them. When she saw they did not eat, she laid her paws, first on one, then on the other, and tried to raise them up, moaning pitifully all the while. She then moved from them, and looked back, and moaned as if for them to follow her. Finding they did not, she returned, smelt them, and licked their wounds; again left them, and again returned; and with signs of inexpressible fondness, went round them, pawing and moaning. At length she raised her head towards the ship, and uttered a growl of despair, when a volley of musket-balls killed her."

despised,—that nothing is without its use,—nothing without its appropriate talent and excellence.*

> ———" 'Tis nature's law,
> That none, the meanest of created things,
> Of forms created the most vile and brute,
> The dullest or most noxious, should exist
> Divorced from good,—a spirit and pulse of good,
> A life and soul, to every mode of being
> Inseparably linked."

187. Next to humanity to brutes, encourage a constant regard for the feelings of playmates; and especially honour kindness done to the weaker and more defenceless.

> " Oh, there's a wicked little world in schools,
> Where mischief's suffered, and oppression rules;
> Where mild quiescent children oft endure
> What a long placid life shall fail to cure.

---

* A reviewer of Captain Hall's Voyages, in an article published some years ago in the Quarterly Review, observes, " We all talk of the ass as the stupidest of the browsers of the field; yet if any one shuts up a donkey in the same enclosure with half a dozen horses of the finest blood, and the party escape, it is infallibly the poor donkey that has led the way. It is he alone that penetrates the secret of the bolt and latch. Often have we stood at the other side of a hedge, contemplating a whole troop of brood mares and their offspring, patiently waiting while the donkey was snuffing over a piece of work, to which all but he felt themselves incompetent."

>   —— Yon boy behold!
> How hot the vengeance of a heart so cold!
> See how he beats, whom he had just reviled,
> And made rebellious, that imploring child:
> How fierce his eye, how merciless his blows,
> And how his anger on his insult grows.*

Such practices, I know, are commonly supposed to belong exclusively to schools for children of the higher ranks; but it is not so. There are little tyrants in rags, as well as in " purple and fine linen:" and nothing is more mysterious than the terror with which these young monsters can sometimes inspire their victims; so that a child will often endure for months, or even for years, a load of exquisite misery, rather than run the risk of incurring, by complaint, some threatened vengeance, with awful ideas of which the tormentor has contrived to fill its excited and morbid imagination. The only security against this evil, is the diffusion of such sentiments in favour of kindness and love as shall render this species of tyranny impossible.

188. BENEVOLENCE may, however, and ought to be manifested, even by children, in other ways besides that of kindness to schoolfellows. A teacher should take care, not only that his pupils sympathise with distress, but that the emotion is followed by efforts for the relief of the sufferer; since, by the production of emotions without corresponding conduct, the character is injured, and a cold and

---

* Crabbe's Tales of the School.

heartless sentimentality induced. Hence it is that fictitious tales of sorrow harden, instead of softening the heart; the moral emotions are unnaturally disjoined from corresponding conduct, and selfishness, instead of being repressed, is cherished. Children are seldom unwilling to aid in the relief of distress. One of our teachers told me, a short time ago, that it was no unusual thing for him, when any child was kept at home, (through the poverty of the parents,) for want of shoes, or other clothing, to mention the circumstance in the school, and that he never did so, without eight, ten, or twelve shillings being contributed the next day. Another informed me, that *in compliance with the proposal of the children,* the boys bring 1*d.* each on the death of the father of any one in the school, which sum is presented to the widow. I could mention many such facts, if it were necessary to do so. These, however, will be sufficient to show, that it is quite practicable thus to form and to foster habits of active benevolence.

189. The inculcation of RESPECT FOR WOMEN, is another branch of civilization, to which, in the education of boys, great attention should be paid. Boys, of the lower classes of society especially, are very apt to treat their mothers and sisters with contempt, merely *as females.* That this feeling is often occasioned by injudicious, and generally ineffectual attempts, on the part of mothers, to make boys the servants of female branches of the family,

there can be no doubt. Against this, nature herself rebels. The great point is to make both parties see their true position, in relation to each other. There is something so graceful and beautiful, in a little sister looking up to a brother as to her natural protector, while she, in turn, full of love and kindness, finds *her* happiness in administering to *his*, that I cannot but think that all the instincts of nature would be on our side, if we did but train them up, *keeping the distinctive position, which God intends the sexes to occupy in relation to each other, always in view.*

190. It is lamentable to think, how few home attachments, how few pleasurable associations, are connected with the fire-sides of the English peasantry. In towns, where the poor are constantly shifting their dwellings, and occupying, at best, inconvenient habitations, in crowded courts and alleys, attachment to *place* cannot be expected; but still, even here, there is room for the love of kindred. Before, however, associations of this cha racter can be expected to exert any considerable influence, a great change must take place, both as to the quality and the quantity of education imparted to the people.

191. In connexion with these efforts to call forth the gentler sensibilities of the mind, *Cherish a taste for the simple and the beautiful.* I take it for granted, that you will devote a few hours, now and then, on a Saturday, to short pedestrian excursions

into the country, with a few of the elder boys. It would be folly to throw away the opportunity which such rambles give for gaining young hearts. Seek then, on such occasions, to open the eyes and ears of your pupils to the sweet sights and sounds of nature. Show them that the richest enjoyments are those which are to be had " without money and without price." Endeavour to make them enter into the spirit of Milton's exquisite lines:—

> " Sweet is the breath of morn, her rising sweet,
> With charm of earliest birds; pleasant the sun,
> When first on this delightful land he sheds
> His orient beams, on herb, tree, fruit, and flower,
> Glistening with dew; fragrant the fertile earth
> After soft showers; and sweet the coming on
> Of grateful evening mild; then silent night,
> With this her solemn bird, and this fair moon,
> And these, the gems of heaven, her starry train."

I press this the more, because a sensibility to the beauties of natural scenery is not common among the poor. It is " a late acquirement of civilized taste." *

192. By these, and a thousand other means, which it is impossible to particularize, you may do

---

* Sir J. Mackintosh. " The perception of excellence is not altogether incompatible with vicious habits, yet few bad men have been distinguished by a nice taste or keen relish for the beautiful and sublime, in nature or in art. These pursuits tend directly to preserve delicacy of feeling, and to cherish the virtuous sensibilities of the heart."

much towards forming a taste for the kind, and the good, and the beautiful, which, if not virtue, is at least highly favourable to its cultivation. I am sure that these powerful influences, secondary* and subordinate as they are, only to the truths of the gospel, have been grievously neglected in elementary schools. If duly cherished, they are capable of being made powerfully subsidiary in the formation of an amiable and elevated character.

193. I know there are some who argue, that this cultivation of the sensibilities, by no means increases the happiness of those who are the subjects of it, since it is impossible to enlarge the inlets of pleasure, without at the same time enlarging also the inlets of pain. The answer of Sir James Mackintosh to an objector of this class, comprises all that can be said in reply. " If the admission of pain be a sufficient objection, it applies with equal force to every degree of thought and feeling; so that it must be better to be an oyster than a man, and a stone than an oyster."

194. The influence of VOCAL MUSIC, in civilizing and humanizing rugged natures, has frequently been adverted to by writers on education. That its importance has been *exaggerated* by some, there can be little doubt; and this very circumstance may,

---

* I say secondary, because the moment they are put in the place of the gospel, they become pernicious. There is a strange tendency to put asunder what God hath joined together.

probably, have induced others to overlook altogether the benefits which may reasonably be expected to follow from its cultivation. Luther, who employed sacred song as a most efficient instrument in advancing the reformation, observes, " It has a mighty control over every movement of the human heart; wherefore I recommend it to every man, particularly to youth, duly to love, honour, and esteem *this precious, useful, and cheering gift of God;* the knowledge and diligent use of which, will at all times *drive off evil thoughts, and diminish the effect of evil society and vices.* It is necessary," he adds, " that this art be taught in schools. A schoolmaster must be able to sing, or else I will not look upon him."

195. The truth is, uncultivated minds, as well as cultivated ones, have their hours of relaxation and of repose, and if these hours be not occupied by some innocent amusement, they will too probably be given up to evil imaginations, to folly, and to vice. In Germany, Switzerland, Holland, and Prussia, a knowledge of vocal music is considered indispensable in a teacher. The minister of public instruction in Prussia, in one of his official documents on this subject, says, " The principal object in teaching music in these schools, is to cultivate the feelings, and exert an influence in forming the habits and strengthening the powers of the will, for which mere knowledge, of itself, is altogether insufficient; hence it constitutes an essential part of

educating instruction, and if constantly and correctly applied, renders the most unpolished nature capable of softer emotions, and subject to their influences." That it has so frequently been made the handmaid of depravity, and the instrument by which the most unholy passions have been fostered and gratified, alone proves the greatness of the power it exercises over the human heart, and impressively teaches the importance of converting it to nobler and better uses. But this can only be effected by forming the youthful taste on purer and better models, and by making that, which is now a rare accomplishment, the property of the people.

196. "We have listened," says a recent traveller in Switzerland, "to the peasant children's songs, as they went out to their morning occupations; and saw their hearts enkindled to the highest tones of music and poetry, by the setting sun, or the familiar objects of nature, each of which was made to echo some truth, or point to some duty, by an appropriate song. We have heard them singing 'the harvest hymn,' as they went forth, before day-light, to gather in the grain. We have seen them assembled in groups, at night, chanting a hymn of praise for the glories of the heavens, or joining in some patriotic chorus, or some social melody; instead of the frivolous and corrupting conversation, which so often renders such meetings the source of evil. In addition to this, we visited communities, where the youth had been trained

from their childhood to exercise in vocal music, of such a character as to elevate, instead of debasing the mind; and have found, that it served in the same manner to cheer their social assemblies, in place of the noise of folly, or the poisoned cup of intoxication. We have seen the young men of such a community assembled, to the number of several hundreds, from a circuit of twenty miles; and instead of spending a day of festivity in rioting and drunkenness, pass the whole time, with the exception of that employed in a frugal repast and a social meeting, in a concert of social, moral, and religious hymns, and devote the proceeds of the exhibition to some object of benevolence. We could not but look back at the contrast presented on similar occasions, in our own country, with a blush of shame. We have visited a village, whose whole moral aspect was changed in a few years, by the introduction of music of this character even among adults; and where the aged were compelled to express their astonishment, at seeing the young abandon their corrupting and riotous amusements for this delightful and improving exercise." The prevailing notion, that vocal music cannot be taught successfully to any who have not *a good ear* for it, is like most other popular errors, a mere fallacy. All who are not destitute of the faculty of distinguishing sounds, may learn it with ease.

197. Last in order here, but first in importance I need scarcely say, in all moral education, is the

inculcation of a regard for TRUTH,—an ardent love for all that is true,—as opposed not only to falsehood and deceit, but to all vain hopes and false valuations. Men do not generally love truth. "This same truth (says Lord Bacon) is a naked and open day-light, that doth not show the masques, and mummeries, and triumphs of the present world, half so stately and daintily as candle-lights. Doth any man doubt, that if there were taken from men's minds, vain opinions, flattering hopes, false valuations, imaginations, *as one would*, and the like *vinum dæmonum*, but it would leave the minds of a number of men, poor shrunken things, full of melancholy and indisposition, and unpleasing to themselves?" Alas, how true! How many, in this way, first dupe themselves, and then become the dupes of others! and what a bearing has this love of delusion, this habit of willing self-deception, on prevailing neglect in matters of infinite moment! How important then is it, that, from the first dawn of reason, the relation which subsists between truth and happiness, delusion and sorrow, should be constantly recognised and impressed! In this respect emphatically

"The child is father of the man."

Where the love of truth is absent, at no period of life can any good eminence be attained, or any true happiness be enjoyed. Lying, is a propensity so demoralizing, and yet so common in children, that the utmost care should be taken to check, and if possible, to eradicate it. The most frequent temptation to falsehood in the young, arises from fear; and is too often occasioned by the violence, and capricious severity, of parents and teachers. This source of evil, I trust, you will avoid. Still you will find it necessary, strictly to watch against even the slightest deviation from truth on the part of your pupils; and when you discover such a departure, the tone and temper of mind in which you reprobate this dreadful habit, should speak volumes to the heart of the offender. *Under no circumstances whatever deceive a child, or tolerate a lie.*

198. I need not enumerate other virtues. The chief point to be remembered by a teacher, in the cultivation of *all* virtue, and in the formation of every good habit, is, that *constant regard must be had to the principle of association.* The power of ASSOCIATION is all but omnipotent in the minds of the young. Sympathy and pleasant associations, have far more influence in determining their habits and preferences, than either argument or persuasion. The great and difficult art is, *insensibly* to introduce into the mind pleasant associations with all that is good, and painful associations with all that is mean, degrading, or sinful. He who has accomplished this, has done much towards "*magnetizing* the mind anew, and calling it out into a fellowship and an existence of a higher order than it had previously owned."

199. I must now briefly refer, to the improvement of what may be termed, the INCIDENTAL OPPORTUNITIES which a school affords, for producing valuable impressions on the youthful mind. These arise from two sources—the position of the teacher himself, *as supreme judge*, and, (in monitorial schools,) the peculiar relation in which a limited number of the pupils stand to him, and to the rest of the scholars.

200. As judge, the teacher presides in what may be termed the ultimate court of appeal; and besides the ordinary direction of the school, many a quarrel and wrong, which could not be decided in the class or the play-ground, comes at length to him. Now the degree of moral influence which a teacher can exercise, will depend very much on the way in which he deals with these cases. Some teachers content themselves, on such occasions, with a rapid and arbitrary decision; and provided they only quiet the parties, and succeed in discouraging such troublesome applications for the future, they do not seem to concern themselves much, as to the absolute value of their judgments. This is wilfully throwing away moral influence. A wise teacher, on the contrary, without encouraging unnecessary and frivolous complaint, secretly hails all these re.erences to himself, as affording the choicest opportunities, not only for exercising the highest and best kind of influence, but for observing the extent to which he has already succeeded in the inculcation of right sentiments, or

the formation of good habits. It is *now* that he can draw the line distinctly between justice and injustice; that he can bring down, even to infantile comprehension, the secret operations of natural selfishness on the heart; that he can exhibit the beauty of meekness, and gentleness, and forbearance, so that it shall be seen and felt; and by a direct appeal to the consciousness of the offending party, make it abundantly evident, that the violence of pride and passion, while it disturbs and destroys the tranquillity of the mind, casts up in its place nothing but " mire and dirt."

201. Monitorial schools, when rightly conducted, are exceedingly favourable to such a course of moral discipline; they alone admit of *the test*, which is requisite, in order to prove that instructions have been regarded. It is true, this holds good only in relation to a certain number of the scholars; but then it must be borne in mind, that in *some* monitorial schools, (those conducted on the plan of the British and Foreign School Society for instance,) this number is not only large, comprising as it does, in one form or other, more than a seventh of the whole, but including just the class of children, in relation to whom it is of the most importance; viz. those who are farthest advanced in knowledge, whether occasioned by the influence of superior intellect, or by longer attendance at the school. To these a TRUST is confided, by which *faithfulness* is tested,—and POWER committed, by which *firm-*

ness and *gentleness* are developed. Continually exposed to bribes, and almost sure of detection if they yield to the temptation, the class becomes to the monitors a school of *integrity*, and a field for the exercise of stern and unbending virtue. Alternately called upon to rule and to obey; surrounded, in both circumstances, by checks, which at once lead to the detection of falsehood and the exposure of tyranny; and ever under the immediate eye and control of superior power; injustice of any kind is easily discovered,—while moderation, humility, truth, and justice, severally find an appropriate sphere and an immediate reward. Where these advantages are not reaped from monitorial government, the fault is not in the system, but in the teacher.

202. The relation which rewards and punishments bear to moral impression, has already been adverted to, in a previous letter. To those remarks I have only one observation to add: *Never deny a child any enjoyment, merely for the sake of accustoming it to contradiction.* You will find abundant opportunity for demanding self-denial, in cases where the wish of the child is opposed to its real welfare, without capriciously thwarting its inclinations, under the pretext of discipline. This mimicry of Providence is not only mischievous—it is wicked. It misrepresents the Divine dispensations, which are never capricious; and it assumes a power, which Infinite Wisdom and Goodness alone is competent to exercise. Never, therefore, deprive

a child of any enjoyment, without a good reason for so doing; a reason which you know would appear satisfactory to a benevolent adult, and which you would explain to the child, if it were not better, for other and more powerful reasons, to withhold the information.

203. Allusion has also been made, more than once, to the necessity of being constantly on your guard against those opposing influences, which are ever at work, resisting, and too frequently counteracting your best endeavours. Parental example is oftentimes one of the most powerful of these antagonist influences with which you have to contend. The education of every child is far advanced before it enters the walls of the school-room. While learning to speak and to walk, the young intelligence has been making observations, and forming habits, and laying up thoughts and feelings, which will exert an influence, more or less powerful, over its whole life. This kind of education is too commonly bad,—thoroughly bad,—and what is worse, it is continually going on. Every day of its life it receives lessons in sin; if not from parents, from friends and acquaintances; at home or in the street; in the field or in the workshop; lessons, which it is but too quick to learn, and which are hardly ever rooted out.

204. To meet this evil, all you can do is, to act as much as possible through the parents, where it is possible to obtain their co-operation. Converse

with them on the peculiar talents and dispositions of their children; try to induce them *to act upon a plan;* and urge the necessity of their exercising care and pains with their offspring, while young, if they would have them made comforts and blessings when they grow old.

205. I know that a great deal of this labour will be thrown away; but that is no reason for withholding it. The truth is, we must be *content* to labour, with the expectation that a great deal of our toil will be in vain. If we cannot agree to this condition of benevolence, we shall do very little good in the world. Let us not forget, that it is a high privilege to be permitted to do any good at all; and let us rest assured, that he who succeeds in throwing one good thought into any one mind, whether it be of a little child, or of an ignorant and careless adult, has not spent a day in vain.

206. This branch of the subject, (the importance of obtaining the co-operation of parents,) recently formed the topic of discussion, at a meeting of British school teachers, at which about seventy assembled. Several interesting facts were then mentioned, one or two of which it may be advisable to record. I give them in the words of the narrators, distinguishing each speaker by a letter of the alphabet.

A. "I have made it a point of duty, ever since I have had a school under my care, to visit as many of the parents as possible, on Saturday mornings. I have found innumerable benefits to result from the practice. I have been able to correct misrepresentations; to remove prejudices; to ascertain the real dispositions of the children; to prevent truant-playing; to check falsehood; and greatly to promote the reformation of notorious offenders. Visits to sick children, I have found eminently beneficial. The parents value these little attentions, and the children are delighted beyond measure. The mother of a sick child told me, that he had been crying for his teacher to come and see him, all the night."

B. "I have frequently been much cheered, by hearing from the parents of the pleasing results of my labours. A few days ago I visited one, who told me he had spent a very dissipated life, until his little boy began to read to him in the evenings. The portions of scripture he thus heard, brought him to reflection, and produced an entire change of character. Another, who had long held infidel principles, had been led to receive the truth, by reading Keith on the Prophecies, which book his child had brought from the school library."

C. "On visiting one of my children, who had been withdrawn from school, I found it was occasioned by afflictions of various kinds, which disabled the parents from paying even the trifle charged. As the boy was remarkably well-behaved, I agreed to take him for nothing. He remained in this way two years, after which I recommended him to a situation, in which he now receives 15s. a-week, and greatly assists his parents. Had I not visited him, he would probably have been left to ruin. In another case, I detected, by visitation, unexpected truancy in two of my eldest boys: I succeeded in bringing them to their knees before their weeping mothers; and they are now thoroughly reformed."

D. "A boy in my school, who I had every reason to believe was a good boy, came to me, and said that he was going to a situation as a cork-cutter on the following Monday, and requested permission to take home his writing-book.

I told him to bring me a note from his grandmother, his parents being dead. He said she could not write. I requested she would call. He brought word that her employment prevented her. From some circumstance or other, I did not visit her; and now I have to confess, that by not doing so, I left him to commit sins, from which I might have saved him. The whole story was a fabrication. The deceit was not discovered for two months, by which time great injury was done to the boy's character. He is now again with me, and the circumstance has taught me a lesson, by which I hope in future to profit."

207. I will only mention one other source of *evil*, against which it is necessary to guard, and that is, THE FLATTERY OF VISITORS. Nothing should be said in the presence of a child which is likely to excite its vanity; and yet, how many persons are indiscreet enough to be continually making observations, in the presence of the young, on the marked superiority, which in some cases they think they perceive, in physical appearance, mental power, or moral development! You cannot always prevent this absurd folly, but you should take immediate steps for counteracting it; not, indeed, by unduly depreciating those who are really superior, but by pointing out, and impressing the obvious truth, that excellence is of various kinds, and that if they have attained it in one branch, others are pursuing it by a different route, and will probably, ere long, equal, or surpass them. Such an occasion should also be seized to remind the pupil, that natural talents, as well as opportunities

for improving them, are the gifts of a Being, who, in his infinite wisdom and goodness, bestows or withholds them, irrespective of personal merits. "What hast thou, which thou hast not received?" is a question which a child can answer; and I know of no more suitable time for asking it, than the hour or moment in which exultation is felt, in the consciousness of intellectual power. At such a period, a delicate reference to the distressing circumstances of idiot children, or to those who are distinguished for remarkable deficiencies in apprehension, may tend, not only to excite humility and gratitude, but also to call forth tender sensibilities towards these weak and afflicted ones.

208. By the diligent pursuit of these means, you will eventually create *a good moral atmosphere* in your school; public opinion will be on the side of virtue; and a majority at least, of the children, will always be ready to assist you in its promotion. Nothing can be of more importance. As it is by moral contagion that vice spreads among the young, rather than by false reasonings or delusive attempts to corrupt, so it is by a like influence of a different character, that virtuous habits are formed and strengthened. A depraved child entering a school, in which this correct tone prevails, will soon find himself obliged, either to withdraw from its influence, or will insensibly become assimilated to its temper and spirit.

209. In order to accomplish all this, however,

you will find it necessary to act systematically. You must *lay down, day by day, your plan of procedure;* and you must so arrange your time, and husband your strength, that not only shall each branch of morals, in turn, come under distinct and specific notice, but that all the machinery of your school, your intellectual exercises, and general arrangements, may work so regularly and easily, that they may facilitate, and not impede, the great end and object you have in view.

210. DIRECT DEVOTIONAL EXERCISES, where the constitution of a school permits the introduction of social worship, may, *under wise direction,* certainly be made productive of great good. But, oh, how much depends upon the manner and spirit in which they are performed! Weariness and disgust, are the least evils that flow from injudicious attempts to impress truth in this way. Habits of sincerity are dreadfully endangered, in any mind which is repeatedly called upon to participate in protracted devotional exercises, unsuited to its capacity, and unadapted to its wants. In such cases, prayer becomes absolutely an evil. Trained thus to formality and hypocrisy, what can be expected, but that children should despise at heart, that which they have long been accustomed to engage in without sincerity or delight?

211. How much deeper is the mischief, if the teacher, entering his school-room with a hurried, disturbed, and angry mind, rushes to devotion as

if it were a matter of school business, and then rising from his knees, vents upon his scholars the ill temper which has been kept back, but not subdued, by the apparent act of worship! Prayer would indeed be a blessing, if the performance of it could insure, during the day, even a moderate share of meekness and consistent piety. I do not scruple to say, that when a teacher does not habitually act in the temper and spirit of devotion, he had far better omit, before children at least, the outward forms of it. It is for this reason, that all legislative enactments as to prayer in day-schools are to be reprobated; and hence the rashness and inconsideration of those, who consider all schools irreligious in which oral prayer is not practised.

212. Whatever difficulties may, however, embarrass the introduction, by a law, of direct devotional exercises in schools, there are none which stand in the way of the teacher's earnest and constant supplication in secret, for a blessing upon those committed to his care; in the absence of which, every effort to affect the heart will be powerless, and every expectation of success vain and delusive.

213. But it is time that I brought this letter to a close; and yet how few and imperfect, after all, are the suggestions it contains, when viewed in relation to the extent and importance of the subject on which it treats! The work is, in fact, gigantic. There is so much to do, that can never be *put down* on paper; so much depends upon seizing

the right moment, and so much upon adapting the mode pursued, to the exigencies of the time, and the disposition of the child; such a nice sense of justice and of propriety, is required on the part of the teacher; so much ingenuousness and benevolence; such unceasing vigilance; such unwearied patience; so much self-government and self-denial; so much tact; such a knowledge of human nature; so much skill in rewarding; so much wisdom in punishing; that I have again and again been led to exclaim, in penning these thoughts, "Who is sufficient for these things?" Under the weight of difficulties so many, and responsibilities so burdensome, a conscientious man could never be sustained, if it were not for the thought, that HE whom we serve, "knoweth our frame, and remembereth that we are dust;" that he kindly accepts the most imperfect services, if rendered in dependence upon him, and with a desire for his glory; and that he will at length say, emphatically, in relation to this service,—" Inasmuch as ye did it unto one of the least of these, my" *little ones,* " ye did it unto me."

LETTER VIII. TO THE SAME.

MORAL AND INTELLECTUAL HABITS OF A TEACHER.

214. I have already attached so much importance to a teacher's embodying in his own character the truths he is endeavouring to inculcate, that I almost feel unwilling again to advert to the subject. But if it be true, that " mothers and schoolmasters plant the seeds of nearly all the good and evil in the world;" if it be the great, the universal law of morals, as well as of physics, that " kind shall bring forth after its kind;" then, since the educator can but reproduce his own image; since good and evil are continually " going out of him;" and by the power of a mysterious assimilation, children become and do, just what he is and does; it is scarcely possible, too frequently or too earnestly to impress upon his mind, that, while no man ministers at a holier altar, no man stands more in need of an enlarged heart and a purified spirit than himself.

215. It is not, however, my intention even to *enumerate*, the various excellences which should adorn the character of the christian teacher. You know the apostolic injunction: — " Whatsoever things are true; whatsoever things are honest; whatsoever things are just; whatsoever things are pure; whatsoever things are lovely; whatsoever things are of good report; if there be any virtue, and if there be any praise, think on these things." (Phil. iv. 8.) Three or four general hints, on the cultivation of habits calculated to insure respect and esteem in the world,—to facilitate the discharge of school duties,—and to aid in the acquisition of useful knowledge,—is all that I ask permission to offer.

216. (1.) *Cultivate diligently the habit of rigid self-control.* He can never rule others successfully, who has not first learned to govern himself. But self-government is a virtue of no easy attainment; implying, as it commonly does, much painful discipline, and sometimes a degree of mental endurance, which the strongest motives alone can enable a man to bear. It must extend, not only to the government of the temper and passions, but to the regulation of the whole conduct: it must determine the distribution of time; the expenditure of money;*

---

* On no account be in debt. Your income, though very limited, is not uncertain: act accordingly. Choose freedom and a crust. Submit to every deprivation, rather than be a *slave.* Debt and degradation are inseparable. A man may

the choice of studies; and the selection both of companions and of amusements; and all this, as I before said, implies painful discipline. Without self-government, however, you can, *as a teacher*, literally do nothing. Where this is wanting, it is obviously impossible to carry out any settled plan, either for our own good, or for the benefit of others. Carried about by every wind of passion, the wretched victim of ill-temper and caprice rejects to-day, that which but yesterday he judged to be above all things desirable; his own irritated spirit kindles irritation in every other bosom; and obstacles, unknown to the tranquil and the meek, block up every avenue to the hearts and consciences of those who are under his control.

217. (2.) *Carefully avoid every thing that is repulsive, even to the most sensitive, either in manner or conduct.* Be neat in your person. A slovenly appearance degrades a man in the sight of the world, and always lessens the respect he receives from children. A man is fearfully mistaken, if he imagines that any strength of mind, or variety of attainments, will excuse vulgarity, rudeness, or dirt. Need I add, *avoid altogether the use of tobacco and snuff?* These habits, to say nothing

---

fawn, or he may be insolent to his creditor,—he is still a slave. If you cannot bring yourself to live within the miserable pittance which a school too often affords, leave it at once, for some other honest calling.

of the expense, which is by no means inconsiderable, or of the injury which they often do to health, which is much more than is commonly suspected, are appropriate only to the ale-house or bar-room; they are but one step above dram-drinking.

218. Let me entreat you also, carefully to guard against the formation of certain *mental* habits, to which your station and employment particularly expose you. You are accustomed to command in the school; and if you do not take great care, you will feel it difficult to brook contradiction out of it. Without incessant watchfulness, you will become arrogant and dogmatic, or pedantic and prejudiced. Such is the natural tendency of constant intercourse with immature minds, looking up to the teacher as an authority. Now all these things are so extremely offensive to intelligent persons, that, if indulged, they will effectually shut you out from society, to which, under other circumstances, you might obtain easy access.

219. *In all your intercourse with your Committee, be modest and courteous.* You must expect to have much to bear from them, especially if they take an active part in the management of the institution. They will occasionally decide on matters they do not at all understand, and perhaps put aside, by a word, plans which have cost you days or weeks of anxious thought to develop. All this is very trying; but there is no remedy for it,

so long as you are under a committee at all. It is impossible to bring any body of men together, to promote a common object, without suffering something from the prejudices and peculiarities which come in with them. If, therefore, they err, or act in a way which you cannot approve, there is but one course for you,—submit cheerfully, or leave their employ. " The obligation of the teacher to yield, is not founded upon the superior wisdom of his employers, in reference to the business for which they have engaged him, for they are very probably his inferiors in this respect, but upon their right, as employers, to determine how their own work shall be done."

220. (3.) *Diligently pursue a regular and systematic course of private study; and let it bear as much as possible upon the duties of your particular profession.* The great object of all education is to prepare for usefulness. Keep this in mind, and read and study simply with the view of thereby obtaining the power to do more good, in the particular position in which Providence has placed you. A teacher who feels aright on this point, will soon see that it is his first duty, to make himself thoroughly acquainted with the *elements* of knowledge. He cannot be content to read or write ill, in order that he may give more time to the mathematics; nor will he consider it any apology for spelling incorrectly, or for being a dull and slow arithmetician, that he is a diligent student

of Latin. A man who acts in this foolish and inconsistent way, (and, alas, there are many,) might learn wisdom from savages. Some Virginian philanthropists once offered to educate a number of the American Indians: they received the following reply:—" Brothers of the white skin, you must know that all people do not have the same ideas on the same subjects; and you must not take it ill, that our manner of thinking, in regard to the kind of education which you offer us, does not agree with yours. We have had, in this particular, some experience. Several of our young men were, some time since, educated at the northern colleges, and learned there all the sciences; but when they returned to us, we found they were spoiled. They were miserable runners; they did not know how to live in the woods; they could not bear hunger and cold; they could neither build a cabin, nor kill a deer, nor conquer an enemy; they had even forgotten our language; so that not being able to serve us as warriors, or hunters, or counsellors, they were absolutely good for nothing." Too many teachers are like these young savages: they may be excellent mathematicians, and good classical scholars; but, alas, they *read* so ill, *write* so carelessly, and are withal so unwilling to stoop to the drudgery of communicating the elements of knowledge, to those who can digest nothing else, that, as teachers in an elementary school, they are absolutely good for nothing.

221. Let it, I pray you, be your first object, to be *thoroughly grounded* in every branch of knowledge you have to teach. The steady, continuous labour, which must be gone through, to know any thing whatsoever thoroughly, is an admirable discipline for the mind. Besides, nothing is so prolific as one thing well known; it is an excellent starting point for a thousand others. Study principles; and never rest satisfied until you are so familiar with every thing you profess, and with the steps by which it must be attained, that you can at once ascertain whether your pupils do, or do not understand what you are communicating,—can discover where their difficulties lie,—can clear up that which is obscure,—illustrate that which is but partially understood,—and present old truths in new and varied aspects. In this way alone, can you ever hope to be an *interesting* instructor. For although it be true, that there must be some natural " aptness to teach," in order to communicate knowledge successfully, yet most persons probably owe more to *culture*, in this respect, than is commonly imagined. No natural talent will enable a man to gain the interest and respect of his pupils so soon, as such a knowledge of his profession, as will enable him quickly to detect an inaccuracy, and to discuss and settle the various questions and difficulties which press upon the mind, and, naturally enough, seem all-important to the pupil. " It is worthy of remark," says Professor Jardine, " that whatever

change for the better shall be made in our systems of education, it must begin with the teachers themselves. The art of teaching, like all other arts, is founded chiefly on experience. Improvements, therefore, are not to be expected from legislators and politicians, who have many other objects to engage their attention; nor even from men of science, unless they have had experience in the business of education. It therefore becomes the duty of every one engaged in teaching, to collect facts, to record observations, to watch the progress of the human faculties, as they expand under the influence of education, and thus to unite their efforts for the general improvement of our academical establishments."

222. *Teaching*, then, should be the object of your constant meditations. It should engage your thoughts by night and by day; and it should regulate, to a very large extent, your private studies:—it should be the end of your labours. The principal reason why there are so few good teachers is, that a school is almost always regarded as a stepping-stone to something else. The hireling fulfils his day, and then hastens to pursuits more congenial to his taste, and destined, he trusts, eventually to deliver him from his present "house of bondage." This is ruinous to success. Ardour and enthusiasm are absolutely necessary to carry a teacher through the drudgery of his duties. He must take pleasure in communicating instruc-

tion to youth; his immediate reward must be their progress; and in the consciousness of discharging one of the most important of all obligations, he must find motives sufficiently powerful to sustain him under exhausting labour.

223. Since, however, the ability to instruct ably in the elementary branches, demands a thorough knowledge of a variety of subjects, it will be desirable, *still keeping in view the advancement of your school*, to pursue a course of study, of a much more enlarged character than would be required, but for its relation to the general discipline and improvement of the mind. It is not perhaps desirable, that I should here attempt to lay down any distinct course of study for your guidance. In deciding upon any given plan, the previous habits of the mind,—the degree of information already possessed,—the natural taste and ability of the student, must all be taken into account. The *essential* literary qualifications of an elementary schoolmaster, at present, are:—1. Good READING. 2. Correct ORTHOGRAPHY. 3. Free and graceful WRITING. 4. A thorough knowledge of ARITHMETIC. 5. An acquaintance with the principles of ENGLISH GRAMMAR. 6. A general knowledge of GEOGRAPHY; and 7. Some acquaintance with ANCIENT and MODERN HISTORY; especially that portion of the former which illustrates the sacred writings, and that department of the latter which relates to our own country.

224. Possessed of these, it will be well for you to turn your attention to the study of THE EXTERNAL WORLD, and to gain such an acquaintance with the animal and vegetable creation, as shall enable you to explain the habits of animals and insects, and the properties of flowers and plants. The elements of NATURAL PHILOSOPHY and of CHEMISTRY should perhaps next gain your attention. High interest may be excited in a school, by familiar explanations of the most common phenomena. GEOMETRY and LINEAR DRAWING, in its various branches, will of course not be neglected. Without a knowledge of the former, you can scarcely proceed a step in science; and the latter is invaluable, were it only as a means of illustration.

225. But the chief object of your study, after all, should be *human nature*, and the laws which regulate and govern the human mind. Study these, not merely as laid down in books, but by a constant habit of observing and analysing character; tracing the motives of actions, both in yourself and in others; and observing conduct, in reference to the moral principles which lie at the foundation of it. Account nothing too minute and trivial for meditation. It is by the frequent contemplation of trivial instances, that great general principles are developed.

226. MENTAL PHILOSOPHY, which, as a science, may be termed " the anatomy of human nature," should be diligently studied by every instructor

of the young. There can be no doubt, that Mr. Dugald Stewart is right, in remarking that " Education would be more systematic and enlightened, if the powers and faculties on which it operates, were more scientifically examined and better understood." For " what," adds he, " is the whole business of education, but a practical application of rules, deduced from our own experiments, or from those of others, on the most effectual modes of developing and of cultivating the intellectual faculties and the moral principles?" Unless you have distinct notions of these faculties, both in their simple and combined forms, and in their mutual influence over each other, I do not see how you can ever pursue any distinct plan for their culture and improvement. This knowledge is, in fact, as essential to you, as an acquaintance with the nature and kinds of the several soils which he endeavours to render productive, is to the intelligent husbandman. Under the most favourable circumstances, you will have much experience to gain at the cost of your pupils; it is therefore of the highest importance, that you should take every precaution to avoid unnecessary mischief. Books on education, involving the application of these principles, will from time to time come under your notice, and these will doubtless be perused with eagerness. But allow me to say, *read them cautiously*. In this department, it is especially necessary to " try the spirits," for " false prophets are gone out into the world." Many a promising volume will not be found to furnish a single hint that is really practical and valuable.

227. *In all your studies, endeavour to cultivate clearness and precision of thought; carefully discriminate between sound and false reasoning; and habitually seek after great general principles.* The habit of expressing the result of your inquiries, in your own words in writing, will be found highly beneficial, in preventing indistinctness and confusion in your ideas; and the immediate impartation to others of that which you have acquired, will, more than any thing else, tend to improve your own mind.

228. In order to the accomplishment of these things, I know that great difficulties must be overcome. Your previous occupations and habits of mind, have perhaps been unfavourable to mental application, and now, the exercise of ATTENTION, (on which every acquisition depends,) is, in any degree of intensity, laborious and painful. Do not, however, be discouraged; by repeated efforts, that which is hard will become easy. *Cultivate the habit of attention.* Be always attentive. If you are *observing* phenomena of any kind, do it carefully,—with your whole mind. If you are reflecting on any subject, be determined to abstract yourself, for the time being, from all external disturbances. In short, whatever you do, " do it heartily;" or, as Lord Brougham has expressed it,

"be a whole man to one thing at once." If you can obtain this kind of mastery over your faculties, you will find it comparatively easy to pass with advantage from one occupation to another; to stop one train of thought, and to commence another; and thus to improve those fragments of time, which otherwise will certainly be lost.

229. Still, with all your care and effort, you must expect to suffer much, not only from that natural restlessness, which belongs to almost every mind which has not been well disciplined in early life, but also from the wanderings of a vain and wayward imagination. The regulation of the IMAGINATION, is so intimately connected with virtuous habits, that, even apart from any considerations connected with the improvement of the intellect, the most anxious attention should be paid to its culture and government. This faculty, which exercises itself in the re-production of past sensations and notions, bringing vividly before the mind both good and evil, in various forms, and combined in every possible variety of manner, tyrannizes over some men with terrible and despotic sway. The objects which in early life have usurped the mind,—the books which have been read,—the trains of thought which have been indulged,—these, constitute the materials, by means of which it creates pictures, reproduces sensations and emotions, recals ideas, and, according to the character of these creations and reproductions, ennobles or contaminates the man. Hence

the importance, not only of habitually controlling the immediate exercise of this imperious faculty, but also of excluding from the mind every thing of a debasing and corrupting tendency. The mischief which is produced by reading immoral writings, for instance, can never be estimated by any immediate result. At the moment of perusal, the mind may be apparently unaffected by the evil with which it is thus brought into contact; other passions or sentiments may be in dominion; a momentary smile is, perhaps, all that has been excited, and the matter is forgotten: the polluted train, of foul images and bad thought, has passed so rapidly along, that it seems as if it had never been. And it is not perhaps till years afterwards, in some hour of sudden temptation, or at some period of that history, which is known only to himself and God, that the delinquent finds out, in all the bitterness of a tortured and agonised spirit, how deep is the injury which he has inflicted on his moral nature, and how difficult he has made the attainment of that purity of heart and mind, after which he now perhaps most intensely longs. This faculty, therefore, must be subjected to severe and constant discipline, if you would attain to any high degree, either of intellectual or moral excellence.

230. All this, I again say, implies labour,—great labour,—and there is no help for it. Labour, is the price God requires us to pay for any earthly good, and we must not grudge the amount. Intel-

lectually, as well as physically, it is the Divine appointment, that man shall earn his bread " by the sweat of his face;" and there is no evasion of this general law. " Without labour and discipline, all direct instruction must be unavailing and useless. The ordinary processes of instruction may put us in a condition for improvement; they may afford us the light of experience to direct our efforts; they may remove unnecessary obstacles from our path; they may point out our defects, and show us the method of correcting them; they may enable us to strengthen what is weak, and to use well what is strong; they may instruct us in the best employment of our faculties; they may teach us how to study, when to study, what to study, and wherefore to study; but after all, study we must, and study is self work, and incomparably the hardest work that is accomplished beneath the sun. The most elaborate and manifold apparatus of instruction, can impart nothing of importance to the passive and inert mind. It is almost as unavailing *as the warmth and light of the sun, and all the sweet influences of the heavens, shed upon the desert sands.**

231. Let me recommend you then, to inscribe over the door of your apartment, the motto of the normal school of Pyritz, in Pomerania, " Pray and work;" a motto, probably suggested by the saying of Luther, " *Bene orâsse est bene studuisse.*" You

* Channing.

cannot stand still. The moment you cease to be a diligent student, your relative position in society begins to alter; others are pressing forward, and if you remain contented with present acquisitions, a few years hence you will find yourself far below your present standing in the community. You have more time for intellectual improvement than falls to the lot of persons in any other employment, and if you do not improve it, you deserve to sink.

232. (4.) *Cherish a kindly feeling towards the young, at all times, and under all circumstances.* Do not attribute to children, dispositions and tendencies which do not belong to them. Many are absolutely discouraged from undertaking any benevolent effort on their behalf, by the frequent complaints which are uttered by teachers, respecting their character and conduct: they are perverse, lazy, thoughtless, ungrateful, and wicked. A well-qualified instructor smiles at these complaints; for he knows that " the teacher is to blame; he is ranking among crimes, actions which are but the unavoidable results of their characters as children; *he is seeking fruit in the time of blossoms.*" Salzmann, to whom I have already more than once referred, insists, that by far the greater number of those faults and defects which grieve the teacher, are but the natural results of his own conduct. Be that as it may, it is certainly of the utmost importance that a teacher should have a good opinion of children; that he should always put the most favourable con-

struction upon their conduct; that he should remember, that children not only do think and act like children, but *ought* to do so; that, in short, he should be fond of them. Cultivate, therefore, a warm interest in their society, and under all circumstances be their friend.

233. (5.) *Studiously avoid every thing which is calculated to impair your health.* Children have no sympathy with morbid affections of the liver and spleen;—an instructor must be cheerful and happy. But cheerfulness depends very much on the state of the body; almost any degree of despondency or irritability may be produced by irregularity of diet, neglect of exercise, or want of sufficient sleep. Take care, therefore, of your health. Beware of late hours. Rise as early as you like, but retire to repose before midnight.

——————————— " Long vigils
Must needs impair that *promptitude of mind*
And *cheerfulness of spirit*, which, in him
Who leads a multitude, is past all price." *

Shun evening teaching. It is impossible that you can do justice to any school, if you teach more than six hours a-day. " A merchant may be employed nearly all the day at his counting-house, and so may a mechanic. A physician may spend all his waking hours in visiting patients, and feel little more than healthy fatigue. The reason is,

* Taylor's Philip Von Artevelde.

that in all these employments, and in fact, in most of the employments of life, there is so much to diversify, so many little incidents constantly occurring, to animate and relieve, and so much bodily exercise, which alternates with, and suspends the fatigue of the mind, that the labours may be much longer continued, and with less cessation, and yet the health not suffer. But the teacher, while engaged in his work, has his mind continually on the stretch. There is little to relieve, little respite, and he is almost entirely deprived of bodily exercise. He must consequently limit his hours of attending to his business, or his health will soon sink under labours which Providence never intended the human mind to bear." *

234. Finally: in all you do, whether relating to the management of your school, or to the regulation of your private studies, ACT UPON A PLAN. Sketch out, every morning, the business of the day, and then pursue the appointed duty with freshness of spirit, with interest, and with hope. You may find it difficult, perhaps impossible, to plan for any extended period, but *plan you must*. Without pre-considered and definite arrangements, you will never be able to conduct satisfactorily the complicated

---

* Where local circumstances render it advisable to establish an evening school, the hours of teaching during the day should be abridged accordingly; for it should be remembered, that a teacher's work is but half done when he has left the school-room.

business of a school, or to pursue with advantage any course of private study.

235. Much more might be added. A thousand suggestions crowd upon my mind, for which I can find no place; suggestions relating to the general discipline of the mind; to the improvement of the faculties; to the attainment of self-knowledge; to the repression of pride, selfishness, and envy; to the cultivation of the devout affections; the quickening of conscience; the cherishing of purity, honour, punctuality, and prudence; the regulation of general reading and conversation; the schooling of the heart; and the absolute necessity of constant dependence on that divine and blessed Spirit, without whose aid even the renewed soul cannot lift its desires and affections heavenward. All this, and much more, should come under notice, were I not checked by the thought, that this species of advice, which would of itself make a volume, has been already offered by others, in every way better qualified than myself to impart such instruction. One word only would I add:—*Let no day pass without spending some portion of your time alone with God.* " An hour of solitude, passed in sincere and earnest prayer, or in conflict with, and conquest over a single passion, or ' subtle bosom sin,' will teach more of thought, will more effectually awaken the *faculty*, and form the *habit* of reflection, than a year's study in the schools without them."*

* Coleridge.

LETTER IX. TO A FRIEND.

DUTIES OF A SCHOOL COMMITTEE.

236. In compliance with your kind request, I will endeavour, my dear friend, to put down as briefly as I can, the objects for which, as it appears to me, a school committee is appointed, and the duties it is intended to fulfil. These, you will soon see, are neither few nor unimportant, whether considered in relation to the teacher, the children, or the public. I shall refer to them in their natural order.

237. (1.) THE SCHOOL ROOM. The first duty of a committee is certainly to provide a suitable building for the purposes of instruction; a room that is light, dry, warm, clean, and well ventilated. When I think of the damp and unwholesome hovels into which teachers and children are too often crowded, my heart sickens. I know more than one instance, in which a promising teacher has in this way been given up to death, through the apathy and sinful negligence of those, whose duty it was to have exerted themselves on his behalf.

238. But it is not enough, that proper arrangements, in relation to health, are secured in the first instance; care must be taken that this provision is actually made available, and that by frequent and thorough ventilation of the room, every thing is done which can be done, to insure, for all parties occupying it, cheerfulness and activity, both of body and mind. Teachers often neglect this important part of their duty, and, through mere carelessness, allow their schools to become dirty, and even unhealthy. Now a committee should guard against this serious evil, by *insisting* upon the school-room being always kept clean, neat, and in good order; and by making liberal provision for frequent white-washing and painting, as well as for the repair of accidental injury. The *moral* effect of a clean and well-aired room, upon children gathered out of filthy and miserable dwellings, is too important to be disregarded by any who are much concerned for their welfare. In fine weather, teachers should be encouraged to take advantage of the nearest plot of ground, and to carry on there the lessons of the school.

239. (2.) SCHOOL MATERIALS. The purchase of these, at suitable times, and in sufficient quantities, obviously comes next in the order of duty. Some committees are very unwilling to furnish a good supply, even of necessary articles. This is, to say the least of it, *bad policy*. It should, on the contrary, be their business, from time to time, to look

round the school, to see what lessons are dirty and torn,—what slates broken,—what books are wanted,—and to take care that a teacher shall find no apology for neglect in the absence of suitable materials. A few pounds judiciously applied every year in this way, *without waiting for solicitation from the master*, would often do more to stimulate both him and his pupils than any thing else. On the same principle, and for similar reasons, the small sum required for the payment of monitors, and for the purchase of rewards, should be readily and cheerfully granted.

240. (3.) THE TEACHER. Having provided a teacher with the *means* of conducting his school well, it is the next duty of the committee to see that these are faithfully and diligently improved. The first point to be secured from him is *early and regular attendance;* and to this end, the visiting members should occasionally call at the school, a few minutes before nine in the morning, and before two in the afternoon. Irregularity of attendance on his part will be fatal to the efficiency of a school. If the teacher be habitually five minutes too late, the children will, as certainly, be ten or fifteen minutes later. A committee should occasionally take pains to ascertain the habits of a teacher in this respect.

241. The next object to be kept in view is *good order*. There is no difficulty whatever in discovering whether a teacher has, or has not, the entire command

of his school. On this head, nothing short of ocular demonstration should suffice; and if it cannot be afforded, *at will*, a committee may rely upon it there is something wrong. It may always be taken for granted, that where there is imperfect control, but little instruction can be imparted, and no moral influence exercised whatever. Where such a defect is observed, they should at once inquire into the cause; and if it be found to result, as it frequently will, from the partial and defective training of the monitors, they should provide for the emergency. If no other course is practicable, it would be better, that for a few weeks, the mass of scholars should be kept in the school only four hours a-day, and thus two hours be secured for more faithful and individual attention to the monitors, than to allow the defect to continue. By such a course, the whole school would actually receive a greater amount of attention, and derive more improvement, than from a greater number of hours professedly devoted to instruction, but accompanied by distraction and disorder.

242. In connexion with this requirement, however, every thing should be done to *sustain the teacher's authority*. No word of complaint, or expression of disapprobation, should ever fall upon his ear in presence of the children; in *their* eye he should be quite as important a person as any member of the committee; the moment he ceases to be so, his power is in a great measure gone.

It is obvious that *he must be trusted*. If he cannot be allowed to punish, excepting in the presence of the managers, or if it is necessary to determine for him, the nature and extent of the infliction, he is not fit to be a teacher. Under such circumstances, a man almost always resorts to some disingenuous contrivance for attaining his end,—a species of trickery which is both degrading and demoralizing.

243. The third point to be secured is, *adherence to a system*. It is of vast importance to a committee, carefully to guard against rash and hasty innovations. Some teachers are always making discoveries,—metamorphosing their schools, for the purpose of carrying out some new principle,—and ending, as these experiments generally do, in the complete disorganization, if not dispersion, of the pupils. Now, while it is far from desirable, that the committees of schools should generally interfere with their internal management; while they should be careful not to check the enthusiasm which leads to the occasional introduction of a new plan, or the modification of an old one; while they should by no means damp ardour by indifference, or paralyze exertion by minute and vexatious legislation; they should, on the other hand, resolutely oppose every deviation from great general principles, which have been long found to work well; and they should invariably discourage that love of change, which almost always issues in disorder. The impossibility of obtaining a successor to such a teacher, without

an entire re-organization of the school, is a position in which no wise committee would willingly place itself.

244. These objects being secured, if a school is not full, it should be the business of the committee to take such steps as may be necessary for bringing in a supply of children. The inconveniences which result from a school being only half filled, are so many, that every exertion should be made, not only to find occupants for every vacant seat, but to have candidates always in waiting for admission. The best mode of accomplishing this, probably, is the free distribution of papers, notifying the situation of the school, describing the branches which are taught, stating the terms of admission, and inviting all who choose to send their children. The Sunday schools in the neighbourhood should then be visited, in rotation, and the co-operation of the teachers secured; and if these fail, personal application at the houses of the poor should be resorted to. The regular visitation of absentees,—the invariable requirement of the weekly payment, allowing no accumulation of arrears,—the encouragement of the industrious and well-behaved, by suitable rewards,—and the occasional appointment of evening examinations, specially for the parents,—will all tend to promote the same desirable result, and should on no account be neglected.

245. But all is not done, in relation to the teacher, when early attendance, good order, system,

and a full school are secured. He needs SYMPATHY, to bear him through the many difficulties and discouragements, which, under the most favourable circumstances, fall to the lot of every conscientious instructor of the young. Mr. Abbott mentions two sources of trial which he considers peculiar to teaching,—difficulties universally felt by instructors, but not attaching to any other profession. The first is, "*moral responsibility for the conduct of others.*" "It is hard enough," he says, for any one to witness the bad conduct of children, with a spirit unruffled and undisturbed; but for their teacher, it is perhaps impossible. He feels responsible; in fact he is responsible. If his scholars are disorderly, or negligent, or idle, or quarrelsome, he feels condemned himself, almost as if he were himself the actual transgressor."*

* Dr. Mayo, who has appended notes to some portions of "The Teacher," appears to me, in this, as well as in some other places, to have mistaken Mr. Abbott's meaning, and (unintentionally I am sure) to have judged him unfairly. It is not "the fear of man," to which he refers, when he speaks of the instructor's accountability, but the judgment which an enlightened conscience passes upon the manner in which duty has been performed. Mr. Abbott, with all his popularity, has some reason to complain of his English editors and publishers. Several editions of his "Teacher" have been issued, in which the chapter on "Religious Influence" is omitted altogether, and this without any notification to the purchaser. Such practices cannot be too severely reprobated. Dr. Mayo's edition, published by Seeley, is decidedly the best, and I believe the only *complete* one.

The second is, *the immense multiplicity of the objects of his attention and care*, during the time he is employed in his business. His work is made up of a thousand minute particulars, which are all crowding upon his attention at once, and which can only be grouped together and combined to a very limited extent. He *must* be systematic; he must classify and arrange; but after he has done all that he can, he must still expect that his daily business will continue to consist of a vast multitude of minute particulars, from one to another of which the mind must turn, with a rapidity which few of the other employments of life ever demand."

246. There are other causes of despondency, however, which are more or less felt, according to the circumstances and character of the teacher; some, arising from the prejudices of parents, against plans which they do not understand; and others, occasioned by *popular neglect*, affecting, as it often does, not only the teacher's pecuniary circumstances, but that instinctive desire to excel, which is always associated with public notice and approbation, and with a good status in society; to say nothing of the natural despondency which is apt to arise, when no direct or immediate benefit is seen to result from long-continued and severe labour. Mr. Pillans thinks it is not going too far to say, (at least in relation to the north of Britain,) that the opposition of the parents to the schoolmaster is often the most violent, in proportion as he deserves

support and encouragement; for, so wedded are they to old habits and practices, that the favourite teacher is not unfrequently the man who truckles to their prejudices, and persists in all the follies of an exploded system. Teachers on the monitorial plan, have, above all others, reason to complain of these absurd prejudices. It is no uncommon thing for a parent to refuse to send one child to school, because " he is taught by other children;" or to withdraw another, because *he* is employed as an instructor, instead of (as the parent argues) being himself taught by the master.

247. Now it is in the power of a committee, greatly to relieve the mind of a teacher, under these circumstances, by a little kindness and sympathy. They can support his authority with the parents; they can occasionally introduce him, if not to their own circles, to the society of those whose rank in life may perhaps be considered a little above his own; and they can show their disposition to deliver him from pecuniary embarrassment, by availing themselves of every opportunity to obtain the means of affording him a liberal salary. *

---

* If a teacher be really efficient, every exertion should be made to remunerate him properly. The highest interests of the community demand, that a much abler and better instructed class of men should devote themselves to elementary instruction, than are at present engaged in that department of labour; but this can never be accomplished, so long as the

248. With all this, he will still have abundant temptation to depression and weariness. The evil example of parents and friends; the counter-education of the street and the workshop; the habits of self-will and vicious indulgence which are engendered at home; irregular attendance; the continual recurrence of faults which he has long endeavoured to extirpate; the absence, in too many cases, of all co-operation on the part of the natural guardians of the child; and the unjust reproach, not unfrequently cast upon him, for deficiencies in the pupil, which arise from confirmed dulness and stupidity;—these, and a thousand other sources of petty vexation, too minute to be mentioned, but, owing to their continual occurrence, not unimportant in their influence on the temper and spirits, must be expected, under the most favourable circumstances, to irritate and sadden the mind of the conscientious teacher: and these are the things which give him so powerful a

---

remuneration attached to the office is inferior to that which is obtained by intelligent mechanics. In some instances, the admission into schools for the poor, of a class of boys somewhat above the labouring class, at a higher rate of payment, has been found to work well, and considerably to increase the teacher's emolument. Care must however be taken, that, under such an arrangement, no undue advantages are offered to those who pay the higher sum; that no invidious distinctions are made in their classification; and that the number thus received is not allowed to become so large as to interfere with the original object of the institution.

claim on the sympathy and kind attention of those who stand towards him somewhat in the relation of employers.

249. (4.) FINANCES. Arrangements of a financial character are, of course, exclusively under the direction of the committee, and on the energy displayed in this department, much of the prosperity of the school will depend. Some schools are always in debt, simply because their committees make no effort to raise subscriptions. Seldom assembling,—when they do meet, no interest in the work is displayed; examinations of the school are deferred; reports are unpublished; the subscribers, hearing nothing of the institution, one by one fall off; debt accumulates; complaints multiply; and at last, a school, on the erection of which hundreds of pounds has been expended, and which has conferred inestimable benefits on thousands of children, is closed, for no other reason than this,—the parties who have undertaken its management are destitute of any real attachment to the cause of education. Such is the sad history of not a few schools, which once flourished in vigour and efficiency. It is the duty of the committee, therefore, never to rest satisfied until they have brought their financial affairs into a healthy and efficient state.

250. (5.) RESULTS. Let me add, in conclusion, that one of the most important and pleasing duties of a committee should be, *to watch for their reward* in the results of educational labour. For, while it

is perfectly true, that eternity alone can disclose the extent of good which may have been effected, or the amount of evil that may have been prevented, through the agency of any school, it is equally certain, that many indications of usefulness, which now pass unobserved, would, if properly followed out, bring to light results highly satisfactory and cheering. This kind of investigation is equally due to the friends and to the enemies of popular education. The prejudices which still linger in many minds, against the impartation of any extended degree of instruction to the poor,—the fears and doubts of some, and the avowed opposition of others,—ought to be met by something more tangible than the declaration of the general principle, (although authoritative,) that " for the soul to be without knowledge, it is not good." Since it is affirmed, (however insufficient may be the grounds of the affirmation,) that the amount of education imparted in schools for the poor, is now too great for the station of those who receive it; that the labouring classes are thereby rendered wiser than their employers; that the natural order of society is in consequence deranged; and that indolence, conceit, and ambition are developed and fostered, it is the duty of those who advocate the diffusion of knowledge, to collect and classify the many facts which come under their notice, tending at once to disprove this kind of assertion, and to demonstrate an opposite conclusion. The slightest investigation, undertaken with an honest desire to discover truth, will show, that in all well-regulated schools, the children who have been longest on the books, and most regular in their attendance, are those who display the most industry and skill,—are most distinguished by correctness of conduct and a religious spirit,—and eventually prove, in whatever situation their lot may be cast, most valuable to those who employ them.

251. There are three ways in which the results of instruction may be ascertained. First, *periodical examinations, conducted in the presence of the committee.* These should not be too frequent, or they will lose their effect. Once in three months, however, such an examination might be very beneficial; it would not assume the character of an exhibition, and it would enable both the teacher and the committee to detect various little deficiencies, which might not in any other way come under notice.

252. (2.) *Personal acquaintance with, and interest in the welfare of the elder boys.* It is of course impossible, that any member of a committee can become acquainted with the majority of the children in a large school; but no material difficulty stands in the way, to hinder any individual from gaining a considerable knowledge of the tempers, dispositions, and habits of those who remain for two or three years, and consequently receive their entire education in the institution. On the contrary, an

intelligent friend of the poor would find great delight in sometimes taking a class of these children apart, and, without at all interfering with the government of the school, he might spend to great advantage an occasional hour, in questioning them upon some lesson of scripture, or other useful topic; in this way drawing out their views and opinions, he might check that which he deemed erroneous, supply what was defective, and encourage that which was praiseworthy. An interest in their future welfare would thus insensibly spring up, and as a natural result, an influence would be obtained over them, highly important both to them and to society at large.

253. (3.) *Meetings of old scholars.* The practice of assembling, at stated times, scholars who have at different periods been educated in a school, has in several instances been found so very beneficial, that it cannot be too frequently or too strongly recommended. At an annual meeting of this kind, held in the Fitzroy school-rooms, London, on the 1st of November, 1836, fifty persons, (old pupils,) from twenty to thirty-five years of age, assembled, and presented a pair of handsome globes to their beloved schoolmaster, " as a memorial of their gratitude for his past instructions, and of the very high esteem which they cherish for his valuable and continued exertions on their behalf." Another of our teachers, writing to me in relation to this class of lads, says, " I have endeavoured to carry out a

plan for meeting them periodically in a Bible class, and have to some extent succeeded. It would do you good to see about thirty of these youths assembled, some of them nearly twenty years of age. These join in the opening of our Sabbath school. Since the formation of this class, they have raised a library, by their own contributions, to the number of about 130 volumes; and in addition to this they have a sick fund, and a fund which gives them some relief when out of employ. We have also a class of girls, of a similar kind."

254. Nor is this state of things rare. The amount of good feeling in a school, is oftentimes much greater than we are led to anticipate by a superficial glance. Circumstances occasionally develop valuable traits of character in a very gratifying and unexpected way. When the master of the British school at Derby left that town, in February last (1836), to promote education in the Bahamas, the monitors of his school, and a few others, raised a subscription among the boys, and purchased a very handsome day and night thermometer, and a magnet, which they publicly presented to their teacher, as a memorial of their gratitude and respect; while the committee of the school, in like manner, showed their sense of his services, by placing at his disposal, scientific instruments to the value of fifty pounds. Many other such instances might be mentioned. In the month of January of the same year, a teacher from the

Q

Borough road being removed from a small hamlet in Staffordshire, to a school in London, a general subscription was raised in the village, and a tea-service was purchased and presented to him, at a parting meeting held in the school-room. These are triumphs, compared with which the achievements of conquerors are not worthy to be named; and, in the contemplation of this ever-extending result of educational labour, a good man will be willing, in the language of an eminent living orator, " to dig his small allotment in the great field of usefulness, to contribute his little item to the cause of truth and righteousness, and to look for the sum total, as the product of innumerable contributions, each of them as meritorious, and many of them, perhaps, far more important and splendid tha his own."

APPENDIX.

A.

A DAY AT THE BOROUGH ROAD SCHOOL.

FIRST CLASS—THE ALPHABET.

"In this class there were no boys, the alphabet not being taught in the usual way,—a single letter at a time, but in connection with words having a definite meaning; a plan which experience has found to be the best. The second class likewise contained no boys, they having been removed into the third, or words of three letters.

THIRD CLASS—WORDS OF THREE LETTERS.

Monitor. Spell BEE. B ee.—What is a bee? A little insect.—What is it fond of? One boy: Sugar. Another boy: Flowers. We asked what sort of flowers? One boy: I know, only I forget; boys afterwards said, roses, tulips, butter-cups.—What else is a bee fond of, what does it like to do? Work.—How does the bee work? Gathers honey. One little boy repeated, "How doth the little busy bee."—Who ought to work? Every body.—What for? To get their living.—What ought not those to do who are lazy? They ought not to eat.—When do boys work? When they go of errands for their mothers; when they come to school.

CUP. Questioned by the Monitor. What is a cup made of? Gold, silver, china.—Who drinks out of gold cups? The king.—Who drinks out of china cups? The gentlepeople.—Who drinks out of earthenware cups? Poor people.—What is drunk out of cups? Tea, coffee.—Where does tea come from? —Where does coffee come from?—What is the inside of a cup? Hollow.—The outside? Convex.—What is the edge called? The brim.

FOURTH CLASS—WORDS OF FOUR LETTERS.

MIND. Spell mind. What is mind? The thinking part of man.—What is the most important subject we can think about? Religion.—What is religion? Thinking about God and doing his will.—What do you think you ought to do? Pray to him, praise him, keep his word.—What do you mean by keeping his word? Obey what he says.—Where do you find what God says? In the Bible.—What is said there that we ought to do? To love God, to fear him. Another boy: To love our parents, to love one another.—Ought you to hate any thing? Yes, sin.—What is sin? Breaking of God's law. Another: Wickedness.—How could you sin against your father and mother? By not doing what they bid us, not to love them.—Tell me something you might do in school that would be sin. To strike a boy, not mind our monitor.—If a boy was to strike you, what ought you to do? Forgive him.—How often? Always.—Who was struck and would not strike again? Jesus Christ.—Who struck him? The soldiers.—What did Jesus say when he was ill used? Father, forgive them: they know not what they do. What part of the Lord's Prayer speaks of forgiveness? Forgive us our trespasses.

CORN. What is corn? Different kinds of grain.—Name some. Wheat, rye, oats, barley.—What do you make from wheat? Flour.—What of flour? Bread.—How is the flour made? The wheat is ground in a mill.—What turns the mill? Wind, water, horses, steam.—What is made of barley? Malt, beer.—Tell me some kinds of beer. Ale, porter, table beer.—What is the use of oats? To make oatmeal, and to feed horses, fowls, and rabbits.—What do you make of oatmeal? Gruel.

FIFTH CLASS.

(In this class the boys commence reading easy portions of Scripture.)

BOY READS—" For this God is our God for ever and ever; he will be our guide even unto death."

What God is this? Our God.—Is he any other people's God? Yes, those that believe in him.—What are those people called who do not believe in him? Atheists.—What do some people make to worship as a god? Images.—What are these people called? Idolaters, Heathens.—In what parts of the world are people heathen? In China, in Hindoostan.—What are those people called who go to preach the true God? Missionaries.—What did the Jews call God? Jehovah.—What sort of a being is God? He is holy. Another boy: He is wise. Another: He is good, he is omnipotent.—What is that? Able to do every thing.—How long is he our God? For ever and ever.—What has he given for our guide in his will? One boy: The Bible. Another: The commandments. Another: Sent Jesus Christ. Another: Ministers to preach. Another: A church.—What else to act on our minds? The Spirit of truth; Christ, "the true light, that lighteth every man that cometh into the world." Another: The Holy Spirit. Another: The Holy Ghost.—What for? To guide us, to comfort us, to show us we are sinners.

(This class spells words of two syllables.)

SACRED. What is sacred? Holy.—Tell me something sacred? The Bible, the Holy Scriptures, the New Testament. Another boy: The name of God.—Prove that from Scripture? " Holy and reverend is his name:" the name of Christ is holy.—What is said of his name? That every knee shall bow to it.

NOTED. What is noted? Tell me something that is noted? A lion.—What is a lion noted for? For strength, for courage, and for boldness. [answered collectively.]—Tell me of some noted men? One boy: Samson was noted for strength. Another: Moses for meekness. Another: Solomon for wisdom. Another: Job for patience, Nebuchadnezzar for tyranny, Nero for cruelty to the christians.—Tell me some noted places? St. Paul's Cathedral, St. Peter's at Rome.—What is England noted for? For commerce, and for liberty. What is Switzerland noted for? Its mountains.

SIXTH CLASS.

(This class also reads selections from the Scriptures, but of a more advanced kind.)

BOY READS—" Servants, obey your masters in all things, according to the flesh; not with eye service, as men pleasers; but in singleness of heart, fearing God."

What is meant by servants? One who serves another for wages. — What is he called who serves another without wages? A slave.—Is it right that we should serve another without wages? No; " the labourer is worthy of his hire."—What are you to do to your masters? Serve them well in all things.—Are you to obey them in every thing they tell you? No, Yes [hesitation;] A boy: In all lawful things.—Who are masters according to the flesh? Our earthly masters.—Who else is our Lord and Master? Jesus Christ.—What is meant by eye service? Only to work when your master looks at you. —How ought you then to serve your masters? As well when they are not looking at you as when they are.—What is meant by men-pleasers? People who care about pleasing only men.—What is singleness of heart? Having only one motive, and that the right one, the love of God.

(This class spells words of three syllables.)

BOY SPELLS FAITHFULNESS.

Tell me some people who were faithful to God when they were tried? Shadrach, Meshach, and Abednego.—Who else? Daniel.

EMIGRATE. What is it to emigrate? Remove from one country to another.—What are people called who emigrate? Emigrants.—Where do they go to? A colony.—What is a colony? A place peopled by people from another country.—Name some colonies? West Indies, Van Dieman's Land, Pennsylvania.—Who founded that colony? William Penn.—How did he get the land? Bought it of the Indians.—Did all do so who founded colonies? No.—Who did not? The Spaniards.—How did they obtain them? By force of arms.—Was this right? No.—How do you know it was not right? Because Christ would not even let Peter defend him, but made him put up his sword.

FERTILIZE. What is the meaning? To make fruitful.—What is this applied to? The ground.—What makes the ground fertile? Sun and the rain.—What country is very fertile? Egypt.—What is the cause of that? The overflowing of the Nile.

SEVENTH CLASS.

(This class also reads the Scripture Extracts from the Old and New Testament.)

JOHN V.

VER. 39. Search the scriptures; for in them ye think ye have eternal life: and they are they which testify of me.

What is meant by search? To look into, to look after.—What is the scripture? The holy writings.—What are these called? The Bible and Testament.—Who wrote the scriptures? Holy men of God spake as they were moved by the Holy Ghost.—Name some of these? [Most of the writers of the Old and New Testament were here named.]—What difference is there in the holy writings? Some are historical, some prophetical, and some epistolary.—Who wrote most of the epistles? Paul.—What were the scriptures written for? Our learning.—What else? To show the way to eternal life.—What else? " For doctrine, for correction, for instruction in righteousness."—Show me some part of the scriptures that applies to doctrine? Jesus said, " ye must be born again." Another boy: " He that believeth on the Son, hath everlasting life." Another boy: " For he is a propitiation for our sins; and not for our sins only, but for the sins of the whole world;" " He that believeth and is baptized, shall be saved;" " For as oft as ye do eat of this bread, and drink of this cup, ye do show the Lord's death till he come;" " There are three that bear record in heaven, the Father, the Word, and the Holy Ghost; and these three are one." Another boy: "Moreover, whom he did predestinate, them he also called; and whom he called, them he also justified; and whom he justified, them he also glorified.—Tell me some passage that affords reproof? " Lying lips are an abomination to the Lord."—Some passage that speaks of correction and retribution? Ananias and Sapphira struck dead for lying. Eli was suffered to die at the news of the ark being taken, for not correcting his sons. Absalom for rebelling against his father. Herod, for his cruelty, for slaying the children, died miserably. Ahab for coveting Naboth's vineyard. Adam and Eve. Cain was a vagabond.—Some passages that speak of instruction? " Go to the ant, thou sluggard." " Let him that stole, steal no more." " Thou shalt love the Lord thy God with all thy heart. Thou shalt love thy neighbour as thyself."—Did our Saviour ever give any general maxim of instruction? " Whatsoever therefore ye would that men should do to you, do ye even so to them."

SPELLING.

(This class spells words of four syllables and gives the derivations.)

MANUFACTURE. What is manufacture derived from? *Manus*, the hand; *factus*, made.—What does it mean? Things made by the hand.—Tell me something manufactured? Linen, from flax; earthenware.—Tell me some country in which flax used to grow? Egypt.—Does it grow now in England? Yes.—What is flax? A tall plant.—How is it prepared for the purpose of making linen? First by soaking, then by separating the fibres by beating.—What county in England is famous for linen manufacture? Lancashire.—Tell me something else manufactured? [The children here described the process of pin making.]—Are pins always made by the hand? No, by machinery.—What is the place called where machinery makes things? A factory.

EIGHTH CLASS: READING—RELIGIOUS INSTRUCTION.

We now proceeded to the examination of the Eighth Class, or boys who read in the Bible and the Society's book of extracts, in which are comprised the monitors, and from which the monitors are selected. The aggregate number of this class is 230, being nearly half the school. The chapter selected by us was the third chapter of Daniel. The reading, upon the whole, was satisfactory; but in so large a class, as might be supposed, was unequal. I was enabled to ascertain, that those were the best readers who had worked their way regularly through all the lower classes; and the reading of these was such as to leave little to be wished; it was slow, clear, distinct, and natural in tone and manner; as unlike the reading generally, in what are termed charity schools, as can be supposed. After the chapter had been read, we questioned the class, and here subjoin our interrogations and the answers returned.

DANIEL, chap. iii.

What have you been reading? An account of the deliverance of Shadrach, Meshach, and Abednego.—Of what nation were these three persons? Israelites.—Why were they called Israelites? Because they descended from Israel, or Jacob.—When was Jacob's name changed to that of Israel? When he wrestled with the angel.—Who was Nebuchadnezzar? King of Babylon.—Where was Babylon? On the river Euphrates.—Into what part of the ocean does the Euphrates fall? Into the Arabian Gulf.—Do you read of the Euphrates any where else in the Bible? Yes; it was one of the rivers that went through the garden of Eden.—What kind of a city was Babylon? [Here, in reply to numerous questions concerning ancient Babylon, of the prophecies concerning its fall or desolation, of their fulfilment, and of its present state, we received the most comprehensive and satisfactory answers.]—Where were the Jews at the time of this occurrence? In Babylon.—Under what circumstances were they there? They had been taken captives. — Why did God suffer those to be taken captives, to whom he had afforded so many signal deliverances? Because they disobeyed God, and transgressed very much, after the abominations of the heathen. [Here the 14th, 15th, 16th, and 17th verses of the 36th chapter of Chronicles were repeated by several of the class.] — What was the great abomination of the heathens? Idolatry.—Do you recollect whom God called, at some remote period, from the idolatry of the very nation of which you have been reading? Abraham.—What did he say to him? Arise, get thee out of thy country and from thy kindred.—Did the Jews ever before forget God and become idolaters? Yes, several times.—Name some of the instances? One boy: When they worshipped the golden calf. Another boy: When they made their children pass through the fire to Moloch, and worshipped Baal. Another boy: Jeroboam made two calves of gold, and said, Behold thy gods, which brought thee out of the land of Egypt.—Was Jeroboam punished for this? Yes; his hand was withered.—Where did the Jews, in all probability, become acquainted with the worship of a calf? In Egypt.—Why? Because the Egyptians worshipped the ox Apis, their principal god.—Do you know any other nations addicted to idolatry? Yes; the Greeks and Romans.—Who were the principal gods of the Greeks? Jupiter, Mars, Apollo, &c.—Do you know of any other ancient nations idolaters? Yes; the ancient inhabitants of England.—What were their objects of worship? The Sun, Moon, Tuisco, Woden, Thor, Friga, and Saturn, from which are derived our days of the week.—In the homage paid to the idol you have been reading of, who was the real receiver of it? Nebuchadnezzar.—Did all give him this homage? All but the Jews.—Can you tell me the motive of those that accused the Jews? One boy: Envy. Another: Malice.—What is the difference between envy and malice? Envy is, being pained at another's happiness; malice, wishes to deprive him of it.—What does malice lead to? Murder, sometimes.—Give me an instance? Cain and Abel; Joseph and his brethren; and Satan, when he tempted Eve.—Did the malice of the Chaldeans have this effect on Shadrach, &c.? No; because God delivered them.—Why did he deliver them? Because they had faith.—What is faith? Belief and confidence in the promises of God.—What means did God use to deliver them? He sent his angel into the midst of the flame.—Whom did this angel resemble? "The form of the fourth is like the Son of God."—Who is the Son of God? Jesus Christ.—Where did Christ come from? From heaven.—Prove that from scripture? One boy: "Before Abraham was, I am." Another boy: "In the beginning was the Word, and the Word was with God, and the Word was

God." Another boy: "The second man is the Lord from heaven." Another boy: "Jesus said, I came from heaven, not to do my own will." Another: "For by him were all things created that are in heaven, or that are in earth, visible and invisible."—Where did Christ first appear? At Bethlehem.—In what form? He was born of the virgin Mary; he came as a child.—Was it prophesied that he should do this? "Behold, a virgin shall conceive and bear a son," &c. "Unto us a child is born, unto us a son is given," &c.—What did Christ come into the world to do? To save the world.—Give me some passages to prove this? "For God so loved the world, that he gave his only-begotten Son." Another boy: "This is a faithful saying, and worthy of all acceptation, that Jesus Christ came into the world to save sinners." Another boy: "Herein is love, not that we loved God, but that he loved us, and sent his Son to be the propitiation for our sins." Another boy: "All we, like sheep, have gone astray, and turned every one to his own way, and the Lord hath laid on him the iniquity of us all."—Who are sinners? All people. Prove this? "All have sinned, and come short of the glory of God; there is none righteous, no, not one."—Why was it necessary that Christ should come into the world for the salvation of sinners? Because, if he had not died, all mankind must have been lost.—What did Jesus Christ do, then, to save mankind? Died on the cross.—How does his dying on the cross save them? Because he died in their stead.—Prove this from scripture? "For Christ also hath once suffered for sins, the just for the unjust, that he might bring us to God."—But had God nothing to do with man's salvation? "God was in Christ, reconciling the world unto himself, not imputing their trespasses unto them." Another boy: "He made him to be sin for us that knew no sin, that we might be made the righteousness of God in him: whom God hath set forth to be a propitiation, through faith in his blood, to declare his righteousness for the remission of sins that are past, through the forbearance of God."—&c. &c.

B.

GRAMMAR.

MODE OF EXAMINATION.

PSALM I.

VER. 1. Blessed is the man that walketh not in the counsel of the ungodly, nor standeth in the way of sinners, nor sitteth in the seat of the scornful.

What part of speech is blessed? Adjective. — Who is blessed? The man.—What is the verb agreeing with man? Is.—How must a verb agree with its nominative? In number and person.—What is the rule? What part of speech is *that*? Relative pronoun.—What is the antecedent to *that*? Man.—Give me the rule? A relative must agree with its antecedent, with its gender, number, and person.—What is antecedent? Going before.—What part of speech is *walketh*? A neuter verb.—Give some other neuter verbs which imply action? Run, swim, leap, jump, swing.—Why are these neuter verbs? Because the action does not pass to any object; it is confined to the act.—Not? Adverb.—What is the rule for placing it after the verb? Adverbs are for the most part placed before adjectives, after verbs active and neuter, and frequently between the auxiliary and the verb.—In? A preposition.—What is a preposition? A word that relates to a noun, to show the relation between.—What is the? A definite article.—Counsel? Common noun.—What case is this in? Objective. Rule 3, Prepositions govern the objective case. —Ungodly? Adjective.—Where is the noun? Man is understood; the ungodly man.—What case is man in? Possessive. —What puts it in the possessive case? Man.—Why? Because it is the ungodly man's counsel, counsel governs it.—What is nor? A conjunction.—The subject of the verb standeth? Man. —The present participle of standeth? Standing.—The infinitive mood? To stand.—The perfect tense of the potential mood? May or can have stood.—Is it a regular verb? No. —Why? Because it does not form its past tense and past participle by the addition of *d* or *ed*.—What is the past tense? Stood.—The past participle? Stood.—In the third verse it is said, " He shall be like a tree ;" what figure of speech is here used? Simile. — What is a simile? A comparison.—What figure would be made if the word " like" were omitted? A metaphor.—Mention some other figures of speech? Climax, metonymy, hyperbole, prosopopeia, antithesis, irony, paralepsis.—Give an instance of irony? " Rejoice, O young man, in thy youth," &c.—Another? Elijah to the worshippers of Baal.—What is climax? The heightening of all the circumstances of an object or action which we wish to place in a strong light.—Give me an instance? " Who shall separate us from the love of Christ? shall tribulation, or distress, persecution, famine, nakedness, peril, or sword?"—What is a metonymy? A figure by which we put the effect for the cause, or the cause for the effect.—Give me an instance? " If mischief befal him by the way in which ye go, then shall ye bring down my grey hairs in sorrow to the grave."—Where is the metonymy here? Grey hairs for old age.—Another instance? " God shall enlarge Japheth, and shall dwell in the tents of Shem, and Canaan shall be his servant."—Another? For Moses of old time hath in every city them that preach him, being read in the synagogues every sabbath day."—Another? " I am the resurrection and the life."—What is a paralepsis? A figure by which the speaker pretends to conceal what he is really declaring and strongly enforcing.—An instance? " If he hath wronged thee, or oweth aught, put that on my own account: I, Paul, have written it with mine own hand, I will repay it, albeit I do not say to thee how thou owest unto me even thine own self besides."—What is antithesis? A figure by which contrary objects are contrasted, to make them show one another to advantage.—Instance? Solomon contrasts the timidity of the wicked with the courage of the righteous, when he says, " The wicked flee when no man pursueth, but the righteous are bold as a lion."—Another? " A wise son maketh a glad father, but a foolish son is the heaviness of his mother." &c.

QUESTIONS FOR EXAMINATION,

EITHER ORALLY OR BY MEANS OF WRITTEN COMPOSITIONS.

THE OFFICE.

1. What is the popular opinion regarding teaching, and wherein is it defective?

2. Mention those circumstances and states of mind under which a teacher *must* be miserable?

3. State how he may best insure happiness?

4. Show the connexion which subsists between happiness in a school and the cultivation of benevolent sentiments?

5. Is a person properly qualified to become a teacher by the acquisition of science merely?

6. Describe the various kinds of power which may be exercised in a school, with their relative advantages and disadvantages?

7. Mention some of the personal inconveniences which arise from hasty and partial preparation for the work of teaching?

8. What influence may a schoolmaster be expected to exercise over the morals and manners of a community, and in what respect does his influence agree with, and differ from, that of the minister of the gospel?

9. What is the best way of acting in a school, when perplexed by a difficult question from a scholar? and why?

10. In what way can intelligent persons be induced to visit and take interest in schools?

11. Define the word "arbitrary," as used in relation to government, and state why children must be governed on this principle?

12. In what respect should the government of a very young child differ from that of an older one? and why?

13. What should be the primary object of attention in a school? an why?

14. Mention some of the leading points to which attention must be paid, in enforcing authority over numbers?

15. Why is it important to reserve extreme punishments for extraordinary occasions?

16. Define "obedience," as it is to be demanded from a child?

17. By what means may general ascendancy over the young be attained?

18. How may public opinion in a school be made to operate in favour of discipline?

19. Mention some common errors which must be avoided, in order to gain influence over the young?

20. To what cause does Salzmann attribute many of the faults of children?

21. What was Lancaster's leading principle in the government of numbers?

22. How should new scholars be treated?

23. What is to be done with the thoroughly incorrigible?

24. What reason have we for supposing that children naturally love order?

THE MONITORIAL SYSTEM.

25. Name some of the advantages which the monitorial system possesses over other plans of instruction?

26. In what respects are monitors better teachers than adults?

27. What are the views generally entertained in Germany of the monitorial system?

28. What advantages may be expected to result to the monitors themselves from being employed as teachers?

29. What are the qualities which indicate fitness to be employed in monitorial teaching?

30. How can monitors be made to feel the responsibilities of their office?

31. What course of training is best adapted to form a good set of monitors?

32. Under what circumstances **must** monitors, however valuable, be dismissed from their office?

THE ART OF TEACHING.

33. What do the Germans understand by the words Didaktik, Pädagogik, and Methodik?

34. What analogy subsists between the profession of teaching and that of medicine?

35. Mention some cases which lead to the conclusion that children naturally delight in the employment of the intellect?

36. State the respective views of Wood, Pillans, and Jacotot, as to the best method of teaching the alphabet?

37. How should spelling be taught?

38. Mention some rules, by attention to which the reading of children may be improved?

39. What is the great principle to be kept in mind in teaching children to read?

40. What object is to be attained, by the constant interrogation of children in relation to what they have read?

41. What is the chief use of visible illustrations?

42. Against what error is it necessary to guard the young, in all endeavours to explain that which is taught them?

43. To what extent should the practice of explaining the prefixes and affixes of words be carried?

44. What is to be understood by incidental teaching?

45. What errors are to be avoided in communicating this kind of instruction?

46. In what way should children learning to write be classed, and on what grounds?

47. Name some of the chief points to be regarded in teaching writing?

48. What great general principle must be kept in view in teaching arithmetic?

49. By what means should children first be introduced to the practice of computation?

50. In what way is it possible gradually to accustom them to abstract calculations?

51. How can you ascertain whether a child thoroughly comprehends the reasons on which an arithmetical process may be founded?

52. What is the best way of explaining to a scholar the principle on which an arithmetical rule is founded?

53. What evils arise from under-rating the difficulties of pupils?

54. By what means may rapidity be attained in arithmetical calculations?

55. State at length the method pursued at the Borough road in teaching English grammar, and its advantages?

56. What is the best mode of imparting instruction in geography?

57. With what parts of the world should children first be made acquainted?

58. Mention the leading features in Woodbridge's lecture on teaching geography?

59. How did Pestalozzi teach this branch of instruction?

60. To what extent may the general principles he adopted be followed out, in teaching geometry, natural philosophy, linear drawing, or history?

61. Why is it important to form good mental habits?

62. In what way may a habit of inaccuracy affect future happiness and usefulness?

63. Define " association," and state the general principle on which various kinds of associations depend?

64. Mention Dugald Stewart's definition of judgment or reason?

65. Why is a man as answerable for his belief as for his conduct?

66. What is the chief end of instruction, as imparted to the labouring classes?

67. Why is an enlarged course of teaching safer, and better adapted for the mass of our population, than a contracted one?

68. By what rule should a teacher be guided, in selecting the branches of knowledge which he is to impart to his pupils?

69. Mention some dangers which arise from a too ready adoption of new methods?

70. What is the difference between a scheming mind, and a mind fertile in expedients for attaining a given end?

71. Who was Pestalozzi, and what was the leading feature of his system?

72. What are the leading objects proposed to be accomplished at Hofwyl? Who was the founder of that establishment?

73. What is the peculiarity of Jacotot's system?

74. What evils arise to indolent minds from the injudicious use of improved methods?

75. What do you understand by precocity of mind, and to what dangers are precocious children exposed?

76. Who was Zerah Colburn? What instruction may be gathered from his history?

77. In what way may some kinds of religious instruction be rendered injurious to a child?

78. What results might be expected from the diligent study of the philosophy of teaching by all classes?

REWARDS AND PUNISHMENTS.

79. Why is it dangerous to punish children for idleness?

80. Mention Dr. Bryce's sentiments in relation to this subject?

81. Why are rewards necessary in large day schools?

82. Define the word "emulation," and state the conflicting opinions which are held by educators in relation to its use?

83. What is the chief object to be kept in mind in the bestowment of a reward?

84. Why is it dangerous to allow a reward to partake of the character of a payment?

85. What is the nature of self-complacency, and why should it be checked in early youth?

86. In what light ought rewards to be regarded?

87. Should rewards be offered only to a few, or be made sufficiently numerous to be brought within the reach of all?

88. What is the primary object to be secured in the infliction of punishment?

89. What circumstances should be regarded in administering it?

90. What is it that renders punishment effectual?

91. In what cases may the infliction of corporal punishment be justifiable?

92. State Fellenberg's views on this subject? Mention also the opinions of Mr. Wood and of Professor Pillans?

93. What common errors in relation to punishment ought to be avoided?

94. State the substance of Denzel's suggestions on rewards and punishments?

MORAL AND RELIGIOUS INFLUENCE.

95. What influence may the general diffusion of knowledge be expected to have upon the interests of religion?

96. What results may be expected to flow from an educator adopting false and flattering views of human nature?

97. What is the great object to be accomplished in moral education?

98. Is it sufficient to pay attention to the enlightening of the mind in relation to truth? What more can human instrumentality effect?

99. In what respect does the influence of a teacher differ from that of a parent?

100. What is the first point to be regarded in all moral education?

101. By what means may the study of the scriptures be rendered interesting to children?

102. What are the elementary truths of the christian faith, and how may these be most successfully impressed on the minds of the young?

103. By what process is it probable that a child will most easily be convinced of the being of a God?

104. How does Mr. Gallaudet attempt to bring within infantile comprehension the doctrine of the immortality of the soul?

105. What general remark of Mr. Gallaudet, in relation to the instruction of children, is worthy of meditation?

106. At what periods should we avoid urging the claims of religion upon children?

107. What should be our guide in the inculcation of scripture doctrines?

108. How may habits of cleanliness be promoted in a school?

109. In what way can the importance of self-denial and temperance be successfully inculcated?

110. How may habits of economy be formed and fostered?

111. What methods should be adopted for the encouragement of gentleness, and for the repression of cruelty to animals, unkindness to playmates, and disrespect for women?

112. How may habits of active benevolence be developed and encouraged?

113. What plans are best adapted to call forth a sensibility to the beauties of nature?

114. What benefits might be expected to result from the general cultivation of vocal music?

115. How is the science of vocal music regarded by educators in Prussia, and on the continent generally?

116. Is it allowable, under any circumstances, to deceive children? Why not?

117. What is it that chiefly determines the habits and preferences of children?

118. What *incidental opportunities* does a school afford for the production of valuable impressions on the youthful mind?

119. What advantage does a monitorial school possess over others, in testing the extent to which instructions have been regarded?

120. Why is it wrong to deny children any gratification, for the sake of accustoming them to contradiction?

121. By what means may the co-operation of parents in the instruction of the young be obtained?

122. How should the evil effects produced on children by flattery, on the part of visitors, be counteracted?

123. Why is it necessary for a teacher to act systematically in the communication of moral and religious instruction?

124. In what temper and spirit should devotional exercises in a school be conducted? In what respects are they liable to abuse?

MORAL AND INTELLECTUAL HABITS OF A TEACHER.

125. Why is it so essential that a teacher should, above all other men, cultivate habits of self-control?

126. What habits should he avoid? Why?

127. Against what mental habits should he be constantly on his guard? Why?

128. In what relation does a teacher stand to a committee, and what duties arise out of that relationship?

129. On what principle should the private studies of a teacher be regulated?

130. Why is it so important that he should be thoroughly grounded in the elements of knowledge?

131. Why should the art of teaching be a constant subject of meditation and inquiry?

132. What are, at present, the essential literary qualifications of an elementary schoolmaster?

133. What should be the chief object of a teacher's study? Why?

134. What results might be expected to flow from a more diligent study of mental philosophy by teachers?

135. What practice is best adapted to promote clearness and precision of thought?

136. By what means may habits of attention be strengthened?

137. What evils arise from an undisciplined imagination? and why is it so important to exclude from the mind every thing that is corrupting?

138. Mention the motto inscribed over the normal school at Pyritz, in Pomerania, and state why it is adapted to every teacher?

139. Why should a teacher have a good opinion of children, as children?

140. What evils are likely to arise in a school, from the health of the teacher being partially impaired?

141. Under what circumstances should evening teaching be avoided?

London:—J. Rider, Printer, 14, Bartholomew Close.

www.ingramcontent.com/pod-product-compliance
Lightning Source LLC
Chambersburg PA
CBHW081325090426

42737CB00017B/3031